Stellar Vibrations:

Living by the Zodiac

Kimberlee Marsh

Kerry Burki

To all you moonbeams out there.
Keep shining your light!

Kimberlee & Kerry

Big love to Rex, Kai, Koda, and Taji. You are my
sun, moon, and stars.
Xo, Kimberlee aka Mom

Matt, Simon, and Isaak, I am so lucky to be in your
orbit. All my love,
Kerry (Mom)

First Edition, 2024

Witch Way Publishing
3436 Magazine Street
#460
New Orleans, LA 70115
www.witchwaypublishing.com

Copyright © 2024 by Kimberlee Marsh & Kerry Burki

Editor: Tonya A. Brown
Cover Designer: Quirky Circe Book Designs
Internal Design: Anissa Cosby

All rights reserved. This book or any portion thereof may not be reproduced or used in any manner whatsoever without the express written permission of the publisher except for the use of brief quotations in a book review.

Printed in the United States of America

ISBN Paperback: 978-1-0882-8596-1
ISBN E-Book: 978-1-0882-8601-2

Table of Contents

INTRODUCTION — Page 8

ABOUT THE SIGNS — Page 11

RITUALS — Page 17

CREATING ALTARS — Page 24

CHAKRAS — Page 26

ARIES — Page 28

TAURUS — Page 36

GEMINI — Page 44

CANCER — Page 52

LEO — Page 60

VIRGO — Page 68

LIBRA — Page 76

SCORPIO — Page 84

SAGITTARIUS — Page 92

CAPRICORN — Page 100

AQUARIUS — Page 108

PISCES — Page 116

LUNAR TABLES — Page 127

INDEX — Page 131

BIBLIOGRAPHY — Page 133

Introduction

This book is about to be your Astrological BFF. It has been specifically created for you to learn about the zodiac, astrological energy, and moon energy in easy and visual ways that will help you expand your understanding and allow you to follow the moon, the stars, and the sun with joy and ease. It will also help you create a life filled with positive and celestial energy.

How to Use This Guide

Below we will guide you through each section and share ways to use this guide as you journey through the zodiac.

Before you dive into each astrological sign, you will be learning about the zodiac, the elements, and the modes. This will help you understand more when you get to each section. You will also be learning about celestial cycles, what they are, and how they play a role in your life.

We want you to start bringing this information into your life, so we have added rituals to practice when the new and full moon are in each sign or anytime you want to bring the energy of that sign into your life. To get started, we share the importance of rituals, how to open and close your ritual space, and how to set up an altar.

For each astrological sign, you will learn about:

- **Mode** – Each sign has a specific mode (cardinal, fixed or mutable)– which defines the energy of the sign.
- **Element** – You will explore which element the sign is associated with. This will give you an idea of the energy to expect during that astrological season.
- **Dates** – The dates shared are when the sun moves into and out of each sign. When it is "Aries Season", it applies to these dates.
- **Glyph** – These are symbols that have been historically associated with astrological signs. These will come in handy when you start looking at

astrological charts and moon charts.

- **Keywords** – Each sign has certain energies associated with them that can be viewed as both positive and negative. These are great to keep in mind when the sun is currently in that sign or when you want to increase or decrease some of the related energies in your life.
- **Planetary Ruler** – Each sign is ruled by a planet, and this also affects the energy and attributes associated with it. For example, Saturn, also known as Cronos or father time, rules Capricorn which is considered to be the mature patriarch of the zodiac, making responsibilities a priority.
- **Mantra** – This is one empowering sentence that captures the energy of the sign. It is perfect to embody during the season or use when the moon is in that sign or any time you want to embody the energy of the mantra.
- **Symbol** – Each sign is associated with a symbol. For example, Taurus is the Bull and Libra is the Scales. Once again, these are related to the associated energies of each sign and will help you remember the characteristics with more ease.
- **Animal** – In addition to the symbol, each sign is associated with being connected to and ruling a certain animal or species. Capricorn is associated with goats and Pisces with fish. You might like to work with these animals as guides during each season.
- **Tarot** – Because each sign has such distinctive characteristics and energies associated with each one, they have a corresponding tarot card from the Major Arcana in traditional Tarot. You can use this card as a guide for each season or do readings using it as the focal point.
- **Body Parts** – In Ancient times, they associated the body with different astrological signs starting with Aries at the top of the head and ending with Pisces at the feet. They might be areas you want to focus on when the sun is in that sign, or if you are experiencing any issues in a particular area you might like to dive more into the energy of the sign.
- **Colors** – Since each sign has such distinct energies it makes sense that they would have corresponding colors. Look around your home and at your wardrobe. Notice which sign you are connected to the most based on the colors you choose. Bring in more of the colors associated with the energy you want to embody more in your life or during a season.

- **Music note** – Music notes have been associated with each sign of the astrological chart. You might like to play this note while meditating during this season.
- **Chakra** – The chakras are spinning wheels of energy found in your energy body. Each one is associated with certain body parts and characteristics which makes it easy for them to have a corresponding sign. You can work with the chakras by imagining their corresponding color as a ball of light in that area as a form of meditation.
- **Goddess/Archangel/Deity** – Certain goddesses, angels, and deities embody the energy of each sign and are particularly helpful to work with when the sun is in that sign.
- **Flowers, Herbs, and Trees** – Historically, many plants have been associated with different signs. You can bring these into your life as tea, spice, incense, perfume, and more.
- **Essential Oils and Stones** – Each oil and stone chosen for each sign shares a little ritual so you can incorporate them and the energy of the sign into your life.
- **New Moon and Full Moon Ritual** – These are perfect opportunities for you to practice self-care and honor the celestial cycles of each sign. Specific dates can be found in the Lunar Tables section of this book (pg. 127). The dates given for the New Moon Rituals correspond with when the Sun is in a particular sign. During this window of time, the new moon will also occur. The dates given for the full moon rituals correspond with the window of time in which the sun will be in the opposite sign that the full moon will occur in. For example, the new moon in Aries will take place between March 21st and April 19th. During that same window of time, the full moon in Libra will also occur. Six months later, the new moon in Libra will occur between September 23rd and October 22nd, this is the same window for the full moon in Aries. These rituals can also be done any time you want to bring in the energy of that sign.

About the Signs

The Elements

Each sign has an element and mode which further describes the characteristics and tendencies of that sign.

Four elements are used in astrology.

1. **Fire**, which is creative and action-oriented.

2. **Earth**, which is stable and steady.

3. **Air**, which is intellectual and communicative.

4. **Water**, which is sympathetic and perceptive.

The Modes

The three modes used in astrology are cardinal, fixed, and, mutable. They further explain the energetic qualities and traits of the signs.

Cardinal – Initiators. They begin the process by laying the foundation. New construction. Aries, Cancer, Libra, Capricorn.

Fixed – Sustainers. They stabilize and maintain what already exists. Restorers. Taurus, Leo, Scorpio, Aquarius.

Mutable – Modifiers. They alter what exists to adapt to current needs. Remodel/Rebuild. Gemini, Virgo, Sagittarius, Pisces.

Fire

Creative, Energetic, Inspirational, Spontaneous, Impulsive

ARIES	LEO	SAGITTARIUS
Cardinal	Fixed	Mutable

Earth

Physical, Enduring, Methodical, Persistent, Stubborn

TAURUS	VIRGO	CAPRICORN
Fixed	Mutable	Cardinal

Air

Mental, Contemplative, Logical, Mercurial, Scattered

GEMINI	LIBRA	AQUARIUS
Mutable	Cardinal	Fixed

Water

Emotional, Intuitive, Empathetic, Sensitive, Moody

CANCER	SCORPIO	PISCES
Cardinal	Fixed	Mutable

Celestial Cycles

In Astrology, much like in life, change happens in cycles.

The main cycles we follow are the Moon, which revolves around the Earth, and the Sun, which the Earth revolves around. More than any other object in the sky, these two celestial bodies affect us daily!

The Sun is defined in the Merriam-Webster dictionary as, "the luminous celestial body around which the Earth and other planets revolve, from which they receive heat and light." The dictionary tells us we are receiving energy from this stellar radiance. The sun is on a 360-day or one-year cycle because every 30 days it moves through one of the 12 signs of the zodiac, and it takes one year to complete this. Every 30 days, the sun transitions from one zodiac sign into the next, thus beginning a new monthly cycle and new energetic vibrational frequency. As it does this, it is highlighting a different part of our natal chart as well as generating entirely different energetic opportunities. The sun changing signs is like an actor stepping into another role and playing a different character.

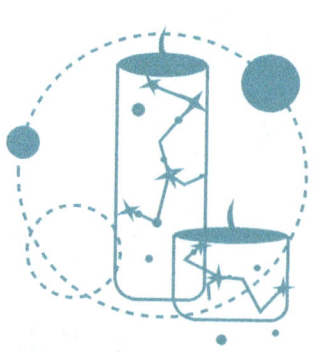

The Moon, whose job it is to reflect the Sun's light, is our closest and most influential celestial body. Earth's very own satellite takes about 28 days to revolve around our planet and changes signs about every two and a half days. The Moon has eight phases each month, yet for this book, we will be focusing on two of them: the new moon and the full moon.

These moon cycles are our monthly opportunities to honor our personal path and connection to the Earth and the cosmos. The new moon happens in whichever sign the Sun is in and is our annual opportunity to honor that aspect of ourselves and to set an intention for a new beginning for that area of our life.

The full moon offers us completion and occurs two weeks after the new moon and will take place in the opposite sign of which the sun is in. Every 28 days there is a new moon which is the coming together of the Sun and Moon in the same sign and degree. And every 14 days after the new moon, there is a full moon, which is when the Sun and Moon are at polar opposites.

Throughout time, these monthly lunar events have been honored by our ancestors as occasions to connect with the divine which was done through various rituals. In this book, you will find that each sign of the zodiac comes with its very own new moon and full moon ritual.

Rituals Make it Real!

Rituals are opportunities to act out our desires and prove to the Universe that we are serious! Not to be confused or grouped with mundane routines; rituals are part of divinity.

What makes something real is the act of doing it.

A funeral honors the dead but it also solidifies the passing for those left behind. It brings closure because it allows the reality of it all to set in. Graduations? Why go through the long and often boring ceremony? It's not required to get your diploma but somehow it makes it real for the graduate.

What do all of these ceremonies have in common? They are rituals that we use in modern society to acknowledge and honor change. Rituals help our brain to understand that a transformation is taking place.

The rituals in this book are designed to keep you in touch with the rhythms of nature and the cycles of the cosmos so that you can stay in alignment with the path of your soul's highest good. The implementation of these rituals do not need to be limited to the new moon and full moon or to the particular sign the Sun is in.

For example, if you have a job interview and want to boost your confidence, you could perform the Aries New Moon Ritual for Personal Power (pg. 34). Or if you find yourself going through a breakup you could do the Libra Full Moon Ritual for Cord Cutting (pg. 82).

These rituals are meant to be used for healing and empowerment and can be used anytime.

Preparing for Your Ritual.

It's important to do a few things as you prepare to enter the realm of the sacred to connect with the spirit of the Earth and with the divine.

The rituals come with supply lists. Don't get stuck on everything having to be perfect. For instance, if the ritual calls for lavender essential oil, but you only have orange essential oil, or for a yellow candle and you only have blue, don't panic. Use what you have.

You will notice most rituals in this book begin with,

"cleanse with your herb bundle and create your sacred space."

You can do this by lighting your herb bundle and allowing its smoke to move around your body to clear your aura of any negative energies.

Almost all ancient cultures use a form of burning herbs to create smoke to cleanse oneself and one's space of negative energy. The burning of white sage has become popularized and commercialized and is considered cultural appropriation. Although we are grateful that folks are reconnecting with their spiritual beliefs aligned with nature, we choose to honor Indigenous Americans by discouraging Non-Indigenous people from using white sage.

The Full Moon in Capricorn Ritual (pg. 106) has instructions on how to create your very own herb bundle for purposes of cleansing with smoke.

Creating your sacred space is as important as cleansing it. Cleansing with your herb bundle rids you and your environment of negative energy and creating your sacred space invites the divine in.

Using smoke and sound to cleanse and bless spaces, purify objects, and send

prayers to the divine has been done in different cultures for centuries. It is a great way to shift the energy of a space from negative or stagnant to positive. Consider doing research on what your ancestors did for cleansing and blessing and bring those into your practice.

Cleanse and Create Your Sacred Space:

For the rituals in this book, you will be cleansing the space around you and the space where you are doing the ritual. You can use smoke or sound to cleanse your space.

Here are some common tools you can use:

- Herb bundles or loose herbs like rosemary, garden sage, and lavender
- Incense
- Frankincense resin
- Singing bowls
- Hand drums
- Chimes
- Hands (clapping)
- Room spray (perfect if you don't like smoke and can't make a lot of noise.)

Before you begin, you will say the following:

"With this smoke/sound/scent, I cleanse this space of any negative, stuck, stagnant, or challenging energy. As I move it around my body and my space, old energy that is no longer serving me is released."

With sound, you can imagine the sound reverberating around and into all the nooks and crannies of your space shaking up and clearing negative or stagnant

energy.

With smoke or spray, you can allow it to move around your body and also bring the smoke into different places in your space. Some people like to move in a counterclockwise motion as they do this.

If you are using an herb bundle or incense, you will carefully light it until there is a flame. Then you will blow it out so that it is smoking. Always be very careful with lit embers and ashes. You might like to use an incense holder, decorative bowl, or similar object to catch ashes. You can also stick incense in a plant pot or a jar with sand. Be mindful to put out your smoke after you are done cleansing or allowing it to burn out with supervision while you are doing the ritual.

Allow the smoke/sound to go around your body and your space, including under chairs, under your bed, in corners, nooks and crannies, and so on.

If you are new to this type of work, play around with what types of smoke and sound you like best to get you started. If you are not new to this work, use your faves and occasionally challenge yourself to find a new sound or smoke to bring into your routine.

After cleansing, you can create sacred space by doing one of the following:
- Imagining white light filling the space.
- Picturing a bubble or angels protecting the space.
- Spritzing with rose water.
- Placing crystals around.
- You can also simply invoke sacred space by saying, "I invoke sacred space."

Once you have completed your ritual, you will need to end it by closing out your sacred space.

We have shared with you an opening and closing invocation which you will find on the following pages.

As with the rituals in this book, feel free to alter them as you desire to make them more personal to you.

Remember, it is the action that makes this real!

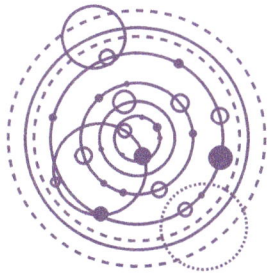

Opening Invocation

Close your eyes and begin to connect with your breath by deepening your inhales and lengthening your exhales. Come into the present moment. Now bring your awareness to your feet and imagine them being connected to the earth beneath you. Allow your feet to keep you grounded knowing that Mother Earth supports you as you begin this sacred ritual.

Repeat:

"I call in my ancestors, my guides, and my higher self to be with me and protect me as I journey into the realm of the sacred.
I acknowledge the four directions, the East, South, West, and North, and the 4 elements they rule, air, fire, water, and earth.
I invite the spirits of plants, stones, and animals to join me in creating this sacred circle outside of time and space where only the truth exists. As I connect with the spirit of nature all around me, my awareness expands, and I become aligned with the celestial beings of the galaxy. I am one with the warmth of the sun, the light of the moon, and the mysteries of the stars above.
I now stand in the sacred space between the worlds."

Closing Invocation

To close out your sacred space, close your eyes and connect with your breath. Feel your heart fill with gratitude.

Repeat:

"I offer gratitude to myself for staying true to my path, for entering this sacred space in order to restore my balance and empower myself to be the best possible version of me.
I thank my ancestors, guides, the four directions, elements, plants, stones, and animals for keeping me safe on my journey. I honor Mother Earth for keeping me grounded and connected to her.
As I open this circle, I will now go forth in joy and gratitude filled with the guidance of the celestial realm."

Creating an Altar for Astrological & Ritual Work

An altar is a space used for focused rituals. Creating one in your home helps give you a sacred space to connect with the divine world. Usually, it is a collection of objects such as photos, statues, candles, incense, matches, crystals, and pretty much anything you desire to add.

You can make your altar a large focal point in a room or create a private one in a small box. There are no rules!

We thought you might like to create altars for each astrological season or when the full moon is in a particular sign. Pretty much any time you want to tap into the energy associated with that sign. Using the information on the first couple pages of each section of the zodiac sign, you can create a beautiful altar that exudes the energy of each sign.

For example, an altar for Cancer season might have:
- The Chariot tarot card
- An image of Selene, the goddess of the Moon, or of the Virgin Mary
- Silver or green jewelry or candles
- Rosemary herb bundle
- Moonstone and/or turquoise stones
- Jasmine or chamomile essential oil
- Moon imagery
- Seashells since it rules shell-covered animals

As you set up your altar, you might like to set the intention of bringing in certain qualities into your life associated with Cancer from the "Keywords" section.

For example: "As I set up my Cancer Season altar, I ask for my home to feel nurturing and safe."

Take some time to feel what it would feel like if your intention was true all the time. You might like to place one hand on your heart and one on your low belly as you do this. (Cancer is connected to the breasts, stomach, and the Sacral Chakra)

Just setting up your altar will help bring in some of those feelings. Then take some time to notice how you can extend those feelings to other parts of your home. Make this your intention for the whole season and notice what ideas pop up and what things related to your intention show up in your life.

You can do this for each astrological season. Have fun with it!

You can also shift items on your altar to use for each of the New and Full Moon Rituals included in each section. You can use the rituals any time you want to tap into the energy associated with each one. For example, any time you want to feel more nurtured, practice the Full Moon in Cancer Ritual (pg. 58).

Allow yourself to have this sacred space for you to connect with your inner self and the ever-changing celestial world.

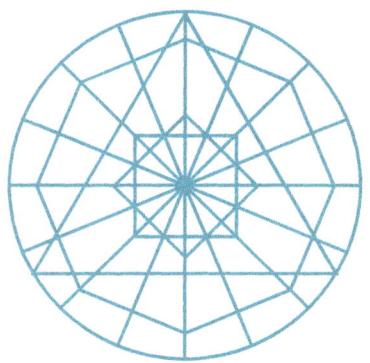

Chakras

	Sahasrara Chakra – Crown – Located at top of head Translates to thousand-petaled. Associated with the Divine and liberations. Thoughts/Consciousness Color: Violet Associated with Pisces
	Ajna Chakra – Third Eye – Located between eyebrows Translates to perceive. Connects us to our intuition and imagination. Light Color: Indigo Associated with Sagittarius and Aquarius
	Vishuddha Chakra – Throat – Located at throat center Translates to especially pure. Associated with speech and expression. Sound Color: Blue Associated with Gemini and Virgo
	Anahata Chakra – Heart – Located at center of chest Translates to unstruck. Associated with love and compassion. Air Color: Green Associated with Taurus and Libra
	Manipura Chakra – Solar Plexus – Located above navel Translates to "lustrous gem." Balance of will and ego. Fire Color: Yellow Associated with Aries and Leo

	Svadhisthana Chakra – Sacral – Located below navel. Translates as "dwelling place of the self." Associated with creativity and sexuality. Water. Color: Orange. Associated with Cancer and Scorpio
	Muladhara Chakra – Translates as Root and Support – Located at base of spine. Connects us to our ancestors and grounds us to Mother Earth. Color: Red. Associated with Capricorn

Aries

THE SIGN OF SELF
MARCH 21ST TO APRIL 19TH
Cardinal and Fire

PASSION ~ BEGINNINGS ~ DETERMINATION ~ WILL
THE FIRST SIGN
RULED BY MARS
SYMBOL – THE RAM
MANTRA = I AM

Keywords:

- Assertiveness
- Sexuality
- Dominance
- Confidence
- Personal Power
- Self Esteem
- Strength
- Anger
- Courage
- Action
- Leadership
- Boldness
- Competitiveness
- Impatience
- Impulsiveness
- Initiating

Aries season is the time of year where you get to exude your personal power and put yourself first. Aries is the first sign of the zodiac and marks the beginning of spring with the Spring Equinox. Being that it is the first sign of the zodiac, it rules the head, face, brain, and eyes. It is the youth of the zodiac and has a "me first" attitude which uses its will for new beginnings.

As a cardinal sign, which is also ruled by fire, it can lead to feelings of confidence and boldness on one hand, and dominance and impulsiveness on the other. Ruled by Mars, the god of war, Aries holds the energy one can use to access their inner power. This connection to inner power stems from the solar plexus chakra, located just below the navel. Due to Mars's fiery passion and tendency to draw blood during battle, the color red resonates with Aries.

Aries, the leader of the flock, is the Latin word for ram and is thus the ruler of sheep. The ram's horns are the symbol and glyph for Aries.

The tarot card associated with this sign is The Emperor. Like the sign of Aries, The Emperor is a confident and courageous leader. He is dressed in his war armor, cloaked with a fiery red robe indicating his readiness to go into battle.

By creating sacred space and lighting a red candle, Astarte, the ancient goddess of war and sexuality can be called upon during this season to help restore your vitality and energy.

Juniper has a history of being used for protection and can be burned as incense during meditation or to cleanse with before going into challenging situations. Red chili pepper can be eaten or placed symbolically on your altar to turn up the heat and get your adrenaline pumping. Thorny trees are representative of Aries, because they were used to draw blood in battle, and should be used with caution.

Honeysuckle is associated with Mars and the beginning of spring. Dab the essential oil on your wrists as a reminder that Aries is the season of new beginnings and to open yourself up to new opportunities. Use several drops of sweet orange essential oil on your solar plexus chakra to balance your inner power.

Garnet's deep red color makes it a perfect match for Aries energy. The stone is known to increase energy and stamina and restore vitality. It also helps to increase one's sex drive.

Pyrite resonates with solar energy and can bring balance to overly emotional or overly aggressive reactions. It aids in grounding and manifestation.

Tarot Card - The Emperor

RULES THE HEAD AND FACE

MUSIC NOTE – E

SOLAR PLEXUS CHAKRA

COLOR – RED

RULES SHEEP AND RAMS

ASTARTE – Light a red candle and call upon Astarte to help restore your vitality and energy.

FLOWERS, HERBS, AND TREES

Juniper, Chili Pepper, All Thorn Bearing Trees

ESSENTIAL OILS

Honeysuckle – Dab on your wrists, rub together, and inhale to open yourself up to new opportunities.

Sweet Orange – Rub several drops on your solar plexus chakra to help balance your inner power.

Combine Juniper and Sweet Orange oils together in a diffuser or spray bottle with water to help restore peace.

STONES

Garnet – Carry with you for extra energy and vitality.

Pyrite – To help manifest your goals into reality, write them down on a piece of paper, fold the paper, and place Pyrite on top.

New Moon in Aries
MARCH 21ST TO APRIL 19TH

Inventory List:

- Herb Bundle – Either store bought or to make your own see Full Moon In Capricorn Ritual Page (pg. 106)
- Crayons and/or markers
- Astromap (pg. 132)

New Moon In Aries Ritual for Personal Inventory

The Aries New Moon marks the astrological New Year and is the perfect time to get back to taking care of number one, you!

To cleanse yourself, light your herb bundle and allow its smoke to move around your body to clear your aura of any negative energies. Then say your opening invocation, see preparing for your ritual and creating sacred space (pg. 19-22).

Get out your crayons and markers and create your own astromap, like the one in the back of this book.

Go through each category and decide how full you are in each area of your life. For instance, if you feel that you are exactly where you want to be in your career and are 100% satisfied, color that area in completely. If you feel you are halfway there, color it in halfway. If you feel like you are far from achieving your goals and haven't accomplished anything in that area, leave it blank.

The point of this exercise is to create a visual map of the areas in your life that may be neglected. Hang this somewhere where you will see it daily.

Come up with the top 3 things that you want to work on and then come up with three actionable ideas for each of them. For instance, if health is an area you feel is neglected, you could:

1. Go for a 20-minute walk 3 times a week.
2. Cut back on sweets in your diet.
3. Make an appointment with your doctor for a physical.

When you have finished, close out your sacred space (pg. 23).

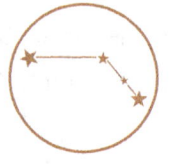

Full Moon in Aries
SEPTEMBER 23RD TO OCTOBER 22ND

Inventory List:

- Herb Bundle – Either store bought or to make your own see Full Moon In Capricorn Ritual Page (pg. 106)
- Red candle
- Citrus essential oil
- Matches or lighter
- Cinnamon tea (your favorite brand or recipe will be perfect)

Full Moon In Aries Ritual to Restore Vitality

Begin by cleansing yourself. Light your herb bundle and allow its smoke to move around your body to clear your aura of any negative energies. Then say your opening invocation, see preparing for your ritual and creating sacred space (pg. 19-22).

Then light your red candle. Anoint your 3rd eye (middle of forehead), wrists, and solar plexus with the essential oil.

Repeat the words:

> "I am a channel for power. Power flows through me. I am powerful."

Now do the following Breath of Fire* exercise for 1 to 3 minutes.
- Sit tall with your palms up on your knees or thighs. Close your eyes.
- Inhale and expand your belly. Exhale and pull in your belly.

Begin to do this at a quick pace with an emphasis on the exhale. The inhale will happen automatically. You will feel this as a pumping sensation above your navel.

- If you are not sure if you are doing it right, try sticking out your tongue and panting like a dog. After a few rounds, continue breathing like that but with your mouth closed.
- To finish, take a deep inhale and hold for a moment or a count of 11 then exhale.
- Then sit for another minute or more, whatever feels best at that moment.

Now drink a cup of cinnamon tea. As it warms your belly, imagine your solar plexus as a large, yellow ball glowing like the sun, expanding until your light from within floods your entire being and begins renewing your life force energy.

Enjoy this feeling.

When you are ready, close out your sacred space (pg. 23).

*Please note that Breath of Fire is not recommended during pregnancy or menstruation. Also, avoid it if you are prone to vertigo or have high blood pressure. Simply do deep belly breathing in and out of your nose.

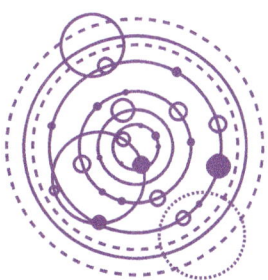

Taurus

THE SIGN OF SELF-WORTH
APRIL 20TH TO MAY 20TH
Fixed and Earth

SENSUALITY - VALUE - FERTILITY - BEAUTY
THE SECOND SIGN
RULED BY VENUS
SYMBOL – THE BULL
MANTRA = I HAVE

Keywords:

- Money
- Perseverance
- Patient
- Steadfast
- Trustworthy
- Resilient
- Determined
- Dependable
- Stagnation
- Possessiveness
- Methodical
- Slow
- Stubborn

Taurus season is a time for slowing down and grounding while allowing for the dust to settle from the remnants of the sun's whirlwind visit through Aries. It offers an opportunity to put impulsive decision-making aside and embrace patience and resiliency. Just be cautious not to waste this fertile energy by getting stuck or caught up in procrastination as your seeds will never grow!

As the second sign of the zodiac, it rules the neck, throat, thyroid, and vocal cords. Taurus, which is Latin for bull is represented by a glyph composed of a circle with an open crescent on top, depicting the bull and its horns and as such rules all forms of cattle.

Since it is the first fixed sign of the zodiac, it is also the most stubborn, however, this is complemented by its belonging to the element of earth which gives the bull qualities of trustworthiness and stability. The planet Venus is the ruler of Taurus as well as the goddess associated with this sign. She further softens what at times can be rather bullish energy by adding elements of sensuality, beauty, and pleasure. With the combination of all of these qualities, Taurus embodies the perfect balance of both masculine and feminine energies.

The shades of light pink and blue correspond to this embodiment by simultaneously creating a spectrum of both coolness and warmth. This same connection to beauty and warmth makes the heart chakra a perfect source of strength for Taurine energy to express itself. The Hierophant is the tarot card that is associated with the sign of the bull. Much like Taurus, The Hierophant is devoted, constant, sensible, grounded, and considered to be a bridge between heaven and earth.

Bathe in heather to inspire feelings of beauty and self-love. Sprinkle some cumin on your food or sip it in your tea to arouse your masculinity. Apples, like the sign of Taurus, are associated with fertility and can be used on your altar as a symbol of both abundance and growth.

Anoint your heart chakra with the essential oil of rose and call upon Venus to help you open yourself to love.

Create a body spray with the essential oil of geranium to restore balance to your masculine and feminine energies.

Tigers Eye can be carried with you to help ground you and make you feel secure. Use aragonite to remain flexible when feeling rigid or stuck.

Tarot Card - The Hierophant

RULES THE NECK, THROAT, AND THYROID

MUSIC NOTE - F

HEART CHAKRA

COLORS - MAUVE AND BLUE

RULES CATTLE

VENUS – Honor your inner Venus and show yourself some love by purchasing your favorite flowers for yourself.

FLOWERS, HERBS, AND TREES

Heather, Cumin, Apple Tree

ESSENTIAL OILS

Rose – Rub on your chest to anoint your heart chakra and call upon Venus to open up to love.

Geranium – Create a body or room spray to restore balance to your masculine and feminine energies.

> Mix 3 parts water – 1 part witch hazel or vodka – 30+ drops of geranium in a glass spray bottle.

STONES

Tiger's Eye – Hold this stone and take deep breaths when you want to feel grounded and secure.

Aragonite – Carry in your pocket or purse during times when you want to remain fluid and flexible.

New Moon in Taurus

APRIL 20TH TO MAY 20TH

Inventory List:

- Herb Bundle – Either store bought or to make your own see Full Moon In Capricorn Ritual Page (pg. 106)
- Lighter or matches
- Pen and paper
- Candle
- Rose essential oil (or an inexpensive rose fragranced oil)

New Moon in Taurus Ritual to Manifest Gratitude

To cleanse yourself, light your herb bundle and allow its smoke to move around your body to clear your aura of any negative energies and say your opening invocation (pg. 19-22) and then light your candle.

Sit still in a quiet space. Close your eyes and focus on deepening your inhales and lengthening your exhales. Now, think about everything in your life that you are grateful for.

Say the words,

"I am grateful for the time and space for this ritual. I am grateful for the support of the earth beneath me. I am grateful for the air I am breathing. I am grateful for my shelter that supports me. I am grateful for the people in my life that bring me joy."

Dig deep and see how many things that you can feel gratitude for in your life.

Once you feel as though you have honored your many blessings with gratitude, begin to think about the things that have not yet manifested in your life, yet you would like to feel gratitude for.

Now, narrow it down to the top three things in which you would like to experience gratitude for. Grab your pen and paper and write,

"I am a source of unlimited supply, with unlimited potential to manifest everything that my heart desires, here and now! As I inhale the future, I exhale the past and make room to experience (write your three desires here) in my life."

Put eight drops of rose essential oil on the paper and use your finger to draw a heart with it. Fold up the paper neatly and close out your sacred space (pg. 23).

Keep the paper with you and read it aloud daily for the next eight days.

On the ninth day, bury it in the earth and prepare to receive all that your heart desires.

 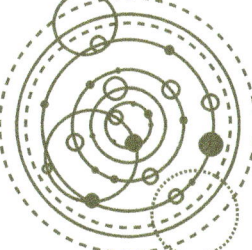

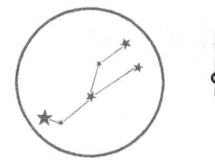

Full Moon in Taurus
OCTOBER 23RD TO NOVEMBER 21ST

Inventory List:

- Herb Bundle – Either store bought or to make your own see Full Moon In Capricorn Ritual Page (pg. 106)
- Lighter or matches
- Large mixing bowl
- Spoon
- Plastic jar or bowl
- Rose essential oil (or an inexpensive rose fragranced oil)
- 1/2 cup of raw sugar
- 1/4 cup of granulated sugar
- 1/4 cup of coconut oil

Full Moon In Taurus Ritual for Self-Love

It's time to treat yourself to some spa pampering.

Begin softening the coconut oil by placing the sealed container of oil into warm water. Place the sugars into your bowl and begin to mix. Slowly add the melted coconut oil and 20 drops of your essential oil while continuing to mix.

Once complete, transfer to your plastic jar or bowl and prepare for your sacred shower.

Begin your ritual by using your herb bundle to cleanse yourself. Light your herb bundle and allow its smoke to move around your body and your bathroom to clear any negative energies. Then say your opening invocation, (pg. 22) for

a suggestion. Once in your shower, use your new scrub all over your body to lavish yourself and your beautiful body.

*Be careful as the oils can cause the tub or shower to become slippery.

Appreciate your unique beauty as you luxuriate in yourself.

Say the words aloud,

"Sugar so sweet, I love myself from my head to my feet. Oil so soft and so smooth, soothe me and invigorate my mood. Heavenly scent of rose, activate sacred love in my heart, let it be all that it knows."

Continue to appreciate your body and all your beauty. When you have finished your shower, close out your sacred space (pg. 23).

Gemini

THE SIGN OF DUALITY
MAY 21ST TO JUNE 20TH
Mutable and Air

COMMUNICATION - MEDIA - INGENUITY - LOGIC
THE THIRD SIGN
RULED BY MERCURY
SYMBOL - THE TWINS
MANTRA = I THINK

Keywords:

- Learning
- Collaboration
- Information
- Writing
- Speaking

- Teaching
- Cleverness
- Siblings
- Neighbors
- Listening

- Neurotic
- Chatty
- Nervous
- Comedians
- Wittiness

Gemini season is the time of year when communication is key and reminds us that it is a two-way street. It is not just about what is said but also how information is received.

Gemini is the Latin word for twins and is the ruler of pairs and duality. Roman numeral II is the glyph for Gemini and represents the twins, Castor and Pollux. It is appropriate that the third sign of the zodiac rule the hands, arms, shoulders, and lungs as they are paired body parts. It is also in charge of the central nervous system and our ability to adapt to change. It rules ideas, thought processes, and expression.

As a mutable sign, which is also ruled by air, it can often feel overwhelmed by too many choices which could lead to nervous tendencies. Ruled by Mercury, the messenger of the gods, Gemini is fast-moving and often erratic, finding difficulties in commitments.

It is fitting that the throat chakra is associated with Gemini and offers the opportunity to speak one's truth. The color yellow is identified with Gemini's originality and inspiration of thought.

The tarot card associated with this sign is the Lovers. Like the sign of Gemini, The Lovers is about the dual aspects found in nature like male and female as well as light and dark. It also presents us with having to make a choice.

The winged goddess, Iris, can be called upon to help you make a choice. Use a yellow marker to write down on a piece of paper what it is you need help deciding. Fold the paper in half and hold it between your hands while saying aloud,

> "Iris, trusted rainbow goddess, take the power of these written words and transform my uncertainty into knowing."

Then bury the paper outside under a rock. On the 2nd day, you will have your answer.

Lily of the Valley can be used to bridge the dichotomy of dark and light. Use caution when handling it as it is poisonous and can be fatal. Dill is known for the clarity of thought and can be sprinkled on your food. Mulberry trees are fabulous for students. The leaves pressed into books are known to increase concentration. Eucalyptus oil can be diffused or rubbed on the throat to activate the throat chakra or inhaled as a vapor to help with troubled breathing. Bergamot oil can be used to make a spray to elevate the mood and aid with clear communication. Azurite's stunning aqua color is the same as the throat chakra and can be placed there to help with speaking one's truth. Amazonite resonates with inner peace and can be placed under your pillow at night to calm a nervous mind.

Tarot Card - The Lovers

RULES THE HANDS, ARMS, SHOULDERS, AND LUNGS

MUSIC NOTE – D

THROAT CHAKRA

COLORS – YELLOW

RULES BUTTERFLIES AND BIRDS

IRIS – The winged goddess can be called upon to help you make a choice.

FLOWERS, HERBS, AND TREES

Lily of the Valley, Dill, Mulberry Trees

ESSENTIAL OILS

Eucalyptus – Diffuse or rub on your throat to activate the throat chakra.

Bergamot – Make a spray or diffuse to elevate mood and aid with clear communication.

STONES

Azurite – Place on your throat chakra to help with speaking one's truth.

Amazonite – Carry it to cultivate inner peace and place it under your pillow at night to calm a nervous mind.

New Moon in Gemini
MAY 21ST TO JUNE 20TH

Inventory List:

- Herb Bundle – Either store bought or to make your own see Full Moon In Capricorn Ritual Page (pg. 106)
- Lighter or matches
- 4 fl. oz. (118 mL) glass spray bottle
- 3 oz distilled water
- 1 oz vodka
- 30 drops bergamot essential oil
- 20 drops of jasmine essential oil
- White label and markers

New Moon in Gemini Ritual for Speaking Your Truth

Begin by cleansing with your herb bundle and creating sacred space (pg 19-22).

Decorate your label with the words, "I Speak My Truth" and other words and symbols you would like your magic potion to help you manifest in the realm of communication in your life.

Once your label is ready, it's time to create your potion. Pour all your ingredients into your glass spray bottle. Tighten the lid and shake vigorously. Make sure the bottle is dry and affix your custom label to it.

As you begin spraying yourself from head to toe with your magic potion, read these words aloud,

"I bless this spray to restore my throat chakra to its proper vibration by transforming anything that might be keeping me from speaking my truth and fully expressing myself. I openly and creatively express myself with truth and integrity because it is my divine right to speak my truth and express myself with confidence and ease".

When you are ready, close out your sacred space (pg. 23).

Continue to use your spray over the next several days and as needed.

Full Moon in Gemini
NOVEMBER 22ND TO DECEMBER 21ST

Inventory List:

- Herb Bundle – Either store bought or to make your own see Full Moon In Capricorn Ritual Page (pg. 106)
- Lighter or matches
- Pen and paper

Full Moon in Gemini Ritual for Making a Decision

Begin by cleansing with your herb bundle and creating sacred space (pg. 19-22).

Pick something in your life that you're having trouble making a decision about and write each of the various options on different pieces of paper. For example, you might be considering moving.

On one piece of paper, you could write, "Move". On another piece of paper, you could write, "Don't Move".

Once you have written down your options, turn the pieces of paper face down and shuffle them to make sure you can't tell which option is which. Then place them on the floor about three feet apart from each other and take turns standing on top of each one. As you stand on each of them, close your eyes and notice what you feel.

Do you feel excited or anxious?

Do any pictures, colors or symbols come to mind?

Spend time on each piece of paper and see which one feels the best.

When you are clear, turn over the paper and you will have your answer! Remember to close out your sacred space when you are done (pg. 23).

 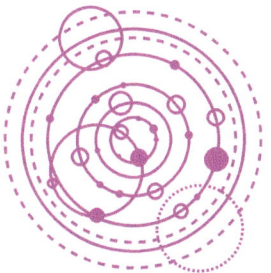

Cancer

THE SIGN OF HOME AND FAMILY
JUNE 21ST TO JULY 22ND
Cardinal and Water

EMPATHY - FEELINGS - FAMILY - NURTURE
THE FOURTH SIGN
RULED BY THE MOON
SYMBOL - THE CRAB
MANTRA = I FEEL

Keywords:

- Home
- Mother
- Safety
- Intimacy

- Moods
- Security
- Insecurity
- Instincts

- Protection
- Tenacity
- Caring
- Possessiveness

Cancer season is the time of year to focus on home and family and can be a great time for nesting, just be cautious not to retreat to the point of becoming a hermit.

Cancer is the fourth sign of the zodiac and marks the beginning of summer with the summer solstice. Aptly, the sign of the mother rules the breasts and stomach. It is the safe place in the zodiac where we go to hide away in the safety of our own home.

As a cardinal sign, which is also ruled by water, it can be protective to the point of confinement. Ruled by the Moon, it is the most emotional sign and can often be moody. The connection to the moon and its cycles links it to motherhood and the sacral chakra, from which life is created.

Silver and green are the perfect colors that resonate with this sign and its watery and fertile nature.

The crab, the symbol for this sign, translates to Cancer in Latin. The crab finds sanctuary in its own shell. The glyph is a number 6 over a number 9 and is said to represent both the eyes of a crab and the breasts of a woman.

The tarot card associated with this sign is The Chariot. Like the crab, the driver of the chariot also has a protective vehicle/ shell to move around in.

When feeling insecure or the need to protect your family, call upon Selene, Goddess of the Moon. After the sun has set, step outside, barefoot under the moon's beams, feel her light shine upon you. Wrap your arms around yourself and say,

"Moon Goddess, light so bright keep me and my family safe tonight."

Daisies have a long history of being associated with newborns. Plant them in the garden before the baby arrives for protection and health. When planted near the front entrance to one's yard, rosemary is said to protect the home and all who live there from harm. Sappy trees are a fitting match for this sentimental sign. Jasmine has long been associated with motherhood and the Virgin Mary. Dab jasmine oil on your pulse points and use it as an aphrodisiac perfume when trying to conceive. The essential oil of chamomile can be diffused or added to a bath to calm the nervous system and reduce anxiety.

Moonstone, with its milky and luminescent appearance, is a stone closely linked to the cycles of the moon and is the perfect remedy to ease into the ever-changing moods of Cancer season. Because of its popularity, it is easy to find already created pieces of jewelry and can be worn to enhance your intuition.

Tarot Card – The Chariot

RULES THE BREASTS AND STOMACH

MUSIC NOTE – G

SACRAL CHAKRA

COLORS – SILVER AND GREEN

RULES SHELL-COVERED ANIMALS

SELENE, GODDESS OF THE MOON – Step outside, barefoot under the moon's beams. Wrap your arms around yourself and say, "Moon goddess, light so bright keep me and my family safe tonight."

FLOWERS, HERBS, AND TREES

Daisy, Rosemary, Sappy Trees

ESSENTIAL OILS

Jasmine – Often associated with motherhood and the Virgin Mary. Dab the oil on your pulse points and use it as an aphrodisiac perfume when trying to conceive.

Chamomile – Diffuse or add to bath to calm the nervous system and induce calm.

STONES

Moonstone – Wear jewelry created with this stone to enhance your intuition and ease into changing cycles and moods.

Turquoise – Wear to stabilize mood swings and bring inner calm and a sense of wholeness.

  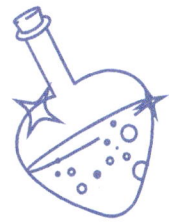

New Moon in Cancer
JUNE 21ST TO JULY 22ND

Inventory List:

- Herb Bundle – Either store bought or to make your own see Full Moon In Capricorn Ritual Page (pg. 106)
- Lighter or matches
- Box of salt
- Bowl or jar
- Flower petals
- Herbs such as tobacco, rosemary, thyme, sage, cumin really whatever you can find in your herb cabinet or from the plants around your garden

New Moon in Cancer Ritual for A Home Blessing

To cleanse yourself, light your herb bundle and allow its smoke to move around your body to clear your aura of any negative energies. Then say your opening invocation, see preparing for your ritual and creating sacred space (pg. 19-22).

Using your herb bundle, you will now set the intention of cleansing any negative or stagnant energy within your home by carrying the smoke into every room, including closets. Be sure to use a fireproof plate to catch any falling ashes.

After this is done, mix the box of salt with your herbs in the bowl or jar. Now pour the contents of the jar around the outside perimeter of your home.

As you do this, say aloud the prayer below to commence your home blessing, making sure to add your own personal touches.

Home Blessing Prayer:

"I call upon the powers that be to bless this home! May this home provide love, laughter, friends, family, prosperity, health, wisdom, and all that my heart desires. Support me as I grow. Provide shelter for me as I prosper. Provide warmth for my friends and family as we celebrate life's triumphs. Provide peace and tranquility for me so I will rest easy. Finally, be my sanctuary that I might retreat to for my peace of heaven. Thank you for these and all blessings. So mote it be."

When you have finished, close out your sacred space (pg. 23).

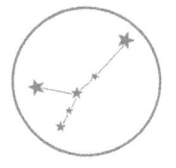

Full Moon in Cancer
DECEMBER 22ND TO JANUARY 19TH

Inventory List:

- Herb Bundle – Either store bought or to make your own, see Full Moon In Capricorn Ritual Page (pg. 106)
- Lighter or matches
- Bathtub or foot soak
- Favorite food
- Favorite flower
- Favorite candle
- Favorite music for relaxation
- Favorite blanket
- Favorite book or movie
- Time and space to take care of you

Full Moon in Cancer Ritual for Support and Security

On the night of the full moon, begin cleansing yourself by lighting your herb bundle and allowing its smoke to move around your body to clear your aura of any negative energies. Then say your opening invocation, see preparing for your ritual and creating sacred space (pg. 19-22).

Now, light your candle and turn on your music. Then, run your bath water adjusting the temperature to your preference.

Once the bath is ready and before entering, place your hands over the water and say the words,

"I bless this water to absorb anything and everything that is keeping me from living in the security of knowing that I am always supported and provided for."

Place your flower on the side of the tub and begin to soak.

As you begin to soak, allow your body to release any tension you might be holding on to. Close your eyes and know the tub is supporting you while the water is nurturing you. As you relax deeper in the tub, imagine that you are a baby again, back in the womb. You have no worries, there is nothing you have to do. Everything you need is given to you. You are safe. You are secure. You are supported. Relax and let go into this feeling of comfort making sure to take some deep cleansing breaths. When you feel ready, open your eyes and look around as though you are seeing the world for the first time and say to yourself,

"I am always supported and provided for.
There is nothing I need to worry about."

When done soaking, blow out your candle and close out your sacred space.

Get under your favorite blanket and enjoy your delicious food and relax in the comfort of your space knowing that you are secure and have everything you need. Spend the night cozied up enjoying your book or movie.

Sleep well!

 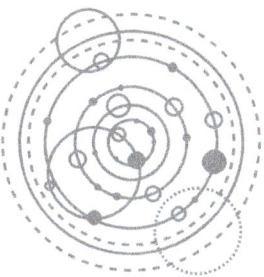

Leo

THE SIGN OF CREATIVITY
JULY 23rd - AUGUST 20th
Fixed and Fire

CONFIDENCE - LOYALTY - JOY - PRIDE
THE FIFTH SIGN
RULED BY THE SUN
SYMBOL - THE LION
MANTRA = I WILL

Keywords:

- Vitality
- Bravery
- Dominating
- Pleasure
- Creativity
- Passion

- Games
- Play
- Parties
- Vacations
- Recreation
- Leadership

- Warmth
- Strength
- Growth
- Children
- Romance
- Drama

Leo season is the time of year where you get to let out your inner child and roar like a lion! This fun and playful energy is a great time to plan events with children, a hot date with your lover, or a warm party for your closest friends.

Leos are known to wear their hearts on their sleeve; it is no coincidence that Leo rules the heart, back, and spine. Leo, with its fondness for admirers, is where we find fun and action in the zodiac. Often pride can be a downfall due to its strong desire for being the center of attention.

As a fixed sign, which is also ruled by fire, Leo offers feelings of warmth and generosity to its loyal subject, but watch out because if that loyalty is questioned, it can turn to dominance and drama in a flash.

Ruled by the Sun, the center of our solar system, Leo believes the world revolves around them. This connection to this strong sense of power perfectly links this sign to the solar plexus chakra, located just above the navel. The colors orange and gold represents warm beams of sunshine and the royalty of the crown.

Leo is Latin for the word lion and is thus the ruler of all felines. The glyph for Leo is said to be both the lion's mane and the heart. The tarot card associated with this sign is Strength. The card depicts a woman holding open a lion's jaw. Much like the sign of Leo, this feat takes courage on the woman's part and loyalty from the lion.

Bastet, the fierce Egyptian goddess of the Sun is depicted as a woman with the head of a lioness. She is the quintessence of strength and courage and is the protector of children. To channel your inner lion/lioness, call upon Bastet to give you the warmth of a housecat and the courage of a cheetah as you do 9 rounds of yogic cat and cow.

Sunflowers, known for their ability to capture solar energy, are a fabulous addition to your home or altar to instantly create a joyous atmosphere. Bay laurel can be used in a soup or stew or simply by just burning the leaf to attract or increase romance. Like sunflowers, citrus trees also capture solar energy. Eat an orange to increase feelings of youth and vitality.

Lemongrass has a calming and grounding effect and is a remedy for taming your lion. It can be eaten, made into tea, or used as an essential oil. Grapefruit essential oil is a pick-me-up and can be added to sea salt for a bath/foot soak.

Rubies are said to increase life force energy and passion. They bring balance to the heart chakra, therefore, wearing one close to your heart is most beneficial. Sunstones can be carried in your purse or pocket to help elevate your mood and attract happy encounters.

Tarot Card – The Strength

RULES THE HEART, BACK, AND SPINE

MUSIC NOTE – E

SOLAR PLEXUS CHAKRA

COLOR – ORANGE AND GOLD

RULES ALL FELINES

BASTET, GODDESS OF THE SUN – To give you the warmth of a house cat and the courage of a cheetah, do 9 rounds of yogic cat and cow.

FLOWERS, HERBS, AND TREES

Sunflower, Bay Laurel, Citrus Trees

ESSENTIAL OILS

Lemongrass – Diffuse or inhale to tame your inner lion.

Grapefruit – To increase joy and vitality, mix 20 drops with sea salt for a bath or foot soak.

STONES

Ruby – Wear it as jewelry to increase life force energy and vitality.

Sunstone – Carry with you or place it in your home as a reminder to enjoy life.

New Moon in Leo
JULY 23RD TO AUGUST 20TH

Inventory List:

- Herb Bundle – Either store bought or to make your own see Full Moon In Capricorn Ritual Page (pg. 106)
- Yellow candle
- Markers or crayons
- Pen and paper
- Envelope
- 10 marigold and/or sunflower petals.

New Moon in Leo Ritual to Manifest Desires

To cleanse yourself, light your herb bundle and allow its smoke to move around your body to clear your aura of any negative energies. Then say your opening invocation, see preparing for your ritual and creating sacred space (pg. 19-22).

Light your yellow candle.

Color a big, bright cheerful sun on your envelope. Be like a child and play.

On your paper, write down 8 wishes that you would like to manifest. Put them in the envelope with 10 marigold or sunflower petals.

Seal it up and keep it in a window that receives moonlight. Close out your sacred space (pg. 23).

On the night of the next full moon take it outside and burn it. As it burns, visualize all your dreams coming true.

Then say aloud:

> "Powerful Fire, element of Leo, I command you to transform my desires into reality. Under the light of this full moon, I release anything blocking me from living my dreams here and now. I now accept and embrace all the wonderful gifts the universe is sending my way. And so it is!"

Now, celebrate!

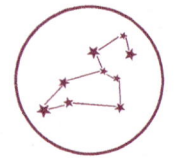

Full Moon in Leo
JANUARY 20TH TO FEBRUARY 18TH

Inventory List:

- Herb Bundle – Either store bought or to make your own see Full Moon In Capricorn Ritual Page (pg. 106)
- Yellow candle
- Matches or lighter

Full Moon In Leo Ritual for Your Inner Child

To cleanse yourself, light your herb bundle and allow its smoke to move around your body to clear your aura of any negative energies. Then say your opening invocation, see preparing for your ritual and creating sacred space (pg. 19-22).

Light your yellow candle and get comfortable in your seat.

Take in some deep cleansing breaths through your nose and begin to gaze at the flame from your candle. Allow your breathing to become natural now as you continue to gaze upon the fire. Watch as the flames dance and flutter as though they were weaving in and out of time. Start to listen with your heart. Bring to your vision memories of when you were just a young child. Look for them in the flame. See them in the flashing light. Remember the time of innocence when your days were filled with play, imagination, joy, and laughter. Invite them to be with you now.

Ask, "How do you feel, my love?" Listen deeply to the voice in your heart. Now that they are here with you and feel safe with you, ask, "Is there an area in

life where I can live in a bigger way to honor both of us?" Listen and look to the flame as reveals the answers you seek.

Once you are clear on where you can be a bigger version of yourself, ask them to join you so that together you can release what keeps you both from living your greatness. And now, give it to the fire.

Watch as the flame ignites and transforms uncertainty into passion. Feel the sparks within you flare up ready to create your biggest life yet. Now return to that sweet little child and say,

"I promise to honor you every day. To remember your innocence, your pure love, joy, and faith in all things. I promise to live in a big way for both of us because I know we deserve and have the right to let our light shine for all the world to see."

With a hug and a kiss, pull them back into your heart. When you are ready, close out your sacred space (pg. 23).

Virgo

THE SIGN OF HEALTH
AUGUST 23rd – SEPTEMBER 22nd
Mutable and Earth

PURITY - HELPFULNESS - INNOCENCE - ORDER
THE SIXTH SIGN
RULED BY MERCURY
SYMBOL – THE VIRGIN
MANTRA = I ANALYZE

Keywords:

- Details
- Health
- Organization
- Service
- Critical Thinking
- Work
- Routines
- Efficiency
- Diet
- Exercise
- Healers
- Perfectionists
- Worry
- Criticism

Virgo season is the time of year where the focus turns to healthy habits and daily routines. It's a sign that is analytical and is great energy for organizing and clearing clutter. There is a danger of this analytical thought process leading to overly critical tendencies towards the self and others.

Virgo is the sixth sign of the zodiac and rules not only one's health but also the work that is done day to day and small animals, like pets. It rules the nervous system and intestines, which can be affected by an overactive mind. It is the helper of the zodiac and lives to be of service. As a mutable sign, which is also ruled by earth, it can be flexible while remaining logical.

Ruled by Mercury, the messenger of the gods, Virgo enjoys communication through organization and details. Like Gemini, the other sign ruled by Mercury, Virgo is also linked to the throat chakra and is concerned with detailed, honest communication. Due to Virgo's connection to agriculture and the harvest, green hues help to define this sign's earthiness.

Virgo, the maiden, is the Latin word for virgin. The glyph for this sign looks like an M and is said to represent the intestines as well as modesty.

The tarot card associated with Virgo is The Hermit. Like the virgin maiden, The Hermit in the Tarot is also thought to be virtuous. The goddess of purity and innocence, Astraea is the patron of this sign and links Virgo to the earth through her devotion to humanity. She was the last of the immortals to walk the planet before her ascent to the heavens to join the other gods. She can be called upon to help with detox and purification.

Valerian can be burned as incense to cleanse your sacred space or taken as an elixir for purposes of detoxification and purification. Bergamot is a mood elevator and aids in communication. It is recommended to use it if Virgo energy becomes too critical. Cedar trees are linked to the summer solstice and are often used for ceremonies and rituals all summer long. It is very appropriate to use cedar in magic work during this time since Virgo is the last sign before the seasons change from summer to fall.

Chamomile is a miracle herb known for its healing qualities. Its ability to calm the mind, settle the nerves and ease digestive issues makes it the very best match for Virgo. It can be taken as a tea, a tincture, or used as an essential oil. Clary sage's earthy aroma has an instant grounding effect when used as an essential oil. It is great to use to come down to earth if the Virgo energy gets too heady.

Moss agate's rich green hues can instantly connect one to Virgo's earth energies. They are known to aid in healing and help with lymphatic flow. All one needs to do to benefit from this healing stone is to simply hold it or place it on the affected areas. Blue lace agate has a calming effect and is said to help ease issues within the throat chakra. Simply place it on your throat and let it work its magic.

Tarot Card ~ The Hermit

RULES THE NERVOUS SYSTEM AND INTESTINES

MUSIC NOTE – G

THROAT CHAKRA

COLORS – GREEN

RULES PETS

ASTRAEA – Call upon her to help with detox and purification.

FLOWERS, HERBS, AND TREES

Valerian, Bergamot, Cedar Trees

ESSENTIAL OILS

Chamomile – Diffuse or apply to wrists and neck to help relieve anxiety.

Clary Sage – Inhale deeply to lower blood pressure and create a calming sensation.

STONES

Moss Agate – Hold in your hand to increase lymphatic flow.

Blue Lace Agate – Place on your throat chakra to activate and heal.

New Moon in Virgo
AUGUST 23RD TO SEPTEMBER 22ND

Inventory List:

- Herb Bundle – Either store bought or to make your own see Full Moon In Capricorn Ritual Page (pg. 106)
- Chamomile essential oil
- Matches or lighter

New Moon in Virgo Ritual Energetic Body Scan

To cleanse yourself, light your herb bundle and allow its smoke to move around your body to clear your aura of any negative energies, see preparing for your ritual and creating sacred space on (pg. 19-22).

Then anoint your 3rd eye, wrists, and throat with the essential oil.

On the night of the new moon, lie down comfortably in your bed and close your eyes. Take several deep breaths until you feel yourself begin to relax.

As you relax, think about a recent event that happened that upset you. Whatever pops into your mind, let it surface. As it is revealed to you, name it. What word describes that feeling?

As you continue to lie peacefully, scan your body and pinpoint where you're holding onto these negative emotions. Start with your head, neck, throat, shoulders, arms, hands, back, chest, stomach, reproductive organs, hips, thighs, knees, legs, ankles, feet, and toes. Once you locate where the emotions are being stored, look

deep within that area of your body.

What do you see? It could be a color, an object, an animal, or a person. Gently begin to remove whatever it is. You may use your imagination or physically use your hands to energetically remove it from your being, directing it to the moon where it can be transmuted. When the area is thoroughly cleansed, fill it with beautiful sapphire blue healing light.

When this is complete, take a final cleansing breath and gently drift to sleep.

Repeat as needed!

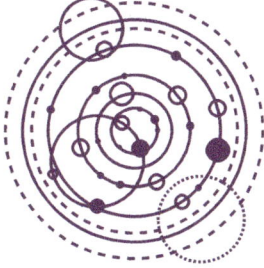

Full Moon in Virgo
FEBRUARY 19TH TO MARCH 20TH

Inventory List:

- Herb Bundle – Either store bought or to make your own see Full Moon In Capricorn Ritual Page (pg. 106)
- Matches or lighter
- Green candle
- Pen and paper
- Clay mud (like Aztec mud)
- Non-metallic bowl
- Non-metallic spoon
- Cedar or sage essential oil.

Full Moon In Virgo Ritual for Body Detox

Begin by cleansing yourself. Light your herb bundle and allow its smoke to move around your body to clear your aura of any negative energies. Then say your opening invocation, see preparing for your ritual and creating sacred space on (pg. 19-22)

Light your green candle. Mix your mud and essential oil in the bowl.

Write down 9 goals that you would like to conquer over the next 2 weeks. These can include beginning a diet and or exercise program, getting health and dental checkups, spa and wellness treatments, getting organized, cleaning, clearing out clutter, and creating a healthy routine.

Once you've written everything down, apply the mud to your entire body. We like

to do this in the shower, tub, or outdoors. As you apply the mud, repeat aloud,

"I honor myself by taking excellent care of my body and mind by making healthy choices."

Once the mud is applied you can leave it on as directed or as long as you're comfortable. As you bask in the mud, know that it is pulling negative toxins out of your body. Think of any negative habits or beliefs that you would like to release. As you rinse the mud off, say aloud,

"Out of my body, out of my mind, negative thoughts and habits have gone forever this time! The mud washes me clean: I now embrace my healthy routine! I begin now my journey of self-love and I seal these words with a powerful self-hug. And so it is!"

When you are ready, close out your sacred space (pg. 23).

Libra

THE SIGN OF BALANCE
SEPTEMBER 22ND TO OCTOBER 22ND
Cardinal and Air

HARMONY - EQUALITY - BEAUTY - PARTNERS
THE SEVENTH SIGN
RULED BY VENUS
SYMBOL – THE SCALES
MANTRA = I BALANCE

Keywords:

- Balance
- Justice
- Diplomacy
- Peace
- Social Gatherings
- Indecision
- Marriage
- Luxury
- Elegance
- Grace
- Codependency

Libra season is the time of year to mix, mingle, and socialize. It is all about relationships, partnerships, and finding the balance between them and you. Libra doesn't want to hurt any feelings and will often compromise its boundaries or become indecisive.

It is the 7th sign of the zodiac and marks the beginning of fall with the autumn equinox, the time of year where we find the perfect balance of day and night. It rules the lower back, butt, and kidneys. It is the sign in the zodiac where we seek justice, diplomacy, and harmony in all relationships.

A cardinal sign, which is ruled by air, Libra can create feelings of righteousness around equality and codependency within relationships. Ruled by Venus, the goddess of love, Libra enjoys beauty, luxury, and grace. Libra holds the energy one can use to access their inner lover and thus links this sign to the heart chakra. The colors of blue and lavender radiate Libra's peaceful and romantic demeanor.

Libra, the sign of justice, is the Latin word for scale and is the ruler of balance. The glyph for Libra is said to be the scale in perfect equilibrium. It is also linked to the Egyptian symbol of the setting sun.

The tarot card associated with this sign is Justice. Like the sign of Libra, the Justice card depicts the scales of balance and equality.

The goddess Aphrodite can aid one with enhancing love, beauty, and romantic relations. On the Friday before the full moon, anoint a blue candle with the essential oil of rose. Carve a heart into it and set your intention.

Roses, sacred to Aphrodite, are a symbol of love and peace. Place them upon your altar to attract more love into your life. Primrose is said to be connected to the divine feminine and is the secret to eternal bliss. Bathing in the herb has long been believed to increase one's beauty and ability to attract a suitable partner. Dogwood trees are associated with the autumn equinox and can aid in keeping diplomatic relations open.

The essential oil of verbena, sacred to many cultures, can be used as an aphrodisiac. Use several drops of rose essential oil on your heart chakra to ease grief and enhance love.

Rose quartz's soft pink color and gentle vibrations help to soothe the heart chakra and restore balance to this energy center.

Jade's green color also connects this stone to the heart chakra and is said to help attract luck in matters of love.

Tarot Card – Justice

RULES THE LOWER BACK, BUTT, AND KIDNEYS

MUSIC NOTE – F

HEART CHAKRA

COLOR – LAVENDER AND BLUE

RULES SNAKES AND LIZARDS

APHRODITE – Can aid with enhancing love, beauty, and romantic relations.

FLOWERS, HERBS, AND TREES

Rose, Primrose, Dogwood trees

ESSENTIAL OILS

Verbena – Diffuse to create an uplifting atmosphere.

Rose – Apply to the chest to open your heart chakra.

STONES

Rose Quartz – Carry with you to soothe your heart chakra.

Jade – Use to attract new love into your life.

New Moon in Libra
SEPTEMBER 22ND TO OCTOBER 22ND

New Moon in Libra Ritual to Celebrate Friendships

In true Libra fashion, it is time to socialize!

On the Friday closest to the evening of the new moon, use this energy to activate your inner Venus and bring people together!

Whether you invite 1 or 10 does not matter, but to keep the balance, make sure you have an even number of attendees!

Libra appreciates beauty and refinement, so pick a place that feels luxurious.

If entertaining from home, spruce up the place ahead of time and create a warm and inviting environment.

Before everyone arrives, write them each a card letting them know that you are grateful for their friendship.

Begin the evening with a toast, honor everyone for gathering and recite the words,

"As we gather, we laugh, we live and we love. Tonight is the night with the blessings from above. Venus looks down upon us with her dedication to pleasure. And in each of you, I find a friendship that I treasure."

Have a blast and enjoy being the god or goddess that is you!

Write down your most cherished friendship memories:

Full Moon in Libra
MARCH 21ST TO APRIL 19TH

Inventory List:

- Herb Bundle – Either store bought or to make your own see Full Moon In Capricorn Ritual Page (pg. 106)
- Matches or lighter
- Candle
- Cord, thread, or yarn
- Scissors
- Cauldron, ashtray, or fire-safe container

Full Moon in Libra Ritual to Cut Cords

Begin by cleansing yourself. Light your herb bundle and allow its smoke to move around your body to clear your aura of any negative energies. Then say your opening invocation, see preparing for your ritual and creating sacred space (pg. 19-23).

Gently tie the cord around your wrist.

Light your candle and take some time to center yourself.

Now, begin to focus on what you want to release in your life. This could be a relationship, bad habit, memory, etc.

Imagine the cord or yarn absorbing all of the energy from which you would like to be released.

When you are ready, cut the cord with your scissors and say the following words aloud.

> "Bound to me no more,
> I am once again free.
> By cutting this cord,
> I banish you from me!"

Now imagine yourself surrounded by white light.

Cleanse the space around you once again with your herb bundle. Burn the cord in your fire-safe container.

You can bury the ashes, flush them or throw them in the garbage. When you are ready, close out your sacred space (pg. 23).

Scorpio

THE SIGN OF TRANSFORMATION
OCTOBER 23RD TO
NOVEMBER 21ST
Fixed and Water

TRANSFORMATION - SEXUALITY - COMMITMENT - POWER
THE EIGTH SIGN
RULED BY PLUTO
SYMBOL – THE SCORPION
MANTRA = I DESIRE

Keywords:

- Inquisitive
- Sexual
- Secretive
- Transformational
- Restoration

- Obsessive
- Suspicious
- Intense Emotions
- Jealousy

- Private
- Empowerment
- Intuitive
- The Underworld

Scorpio season is the time of year when we prepare to enter the underworld. Just make sure not to get stuck there. Scorpio is the 8th sign of the zodiac and marks the beginning of darker days. It rules both male and female reproductive organs and the cycles of death and rebirth. It is a fixed sign and is also ruled by water, which can lead to protective and nurturing energies at best.

When not at its best, Scorpio energy can be possessive, jealous, manipulative, and emotionally intense.

Ruled by Pluto, the god of the underworld, Scorpio holds energies that can be channeled for powerful transformation and rebirth or for destruction. When used properly, this energy can transmute poison and lead to profound healing. Scorpio's rulership of the reproductive organs connects it to the sacral chakra, located just below the navel. Due to Pluto's connection to death and the underworld, black and maroon are the colors that resonate with Scorpio energy. Scorpio is the Latin word for Scorpion, the killer insect, and is thus the ruler of insects. The glyph for this sign is an M with an arrow sticking out of it and it is said to represent both the stinger of a scorpion and reproductive organs.

The tarot card associated with this sign is the Death card. Like the sign of Scorpio, it is concerned with death and the underworld. The card depicts a skeleton on a horse, marking an ending that will soon bring transformation.

Kali, the Hindu goddess of death and destruction resonates perfectly with Scorpio energy. Burn dragon's blood or copal to call upon her for support in times of deep transformation and change.

Marigolds are used in Mesoamerican ceremonies to honor the dead and to welcome them back to earth. The holiday, which occurs during Scorpio season, is called Dia de los Muertos and is when the veil between the worlds of the living and dead is said to be thin.

Dragon's blood is associated with death and transformation and has been used as a form of embalming bodies. The resin has a pleasant grounding aroma, which can be used to welcome transformation. Blackthorn trees are associated with dark magic, which is ruled by Scorpio. Use with caution. Ylang Ylang, which resonates with the sacral chakra, helps balance the energy in the reproductive organs. Use the essential oil in a bath, a diffuser or directly on your skin to stimulate this energy. Sandalwood essential oil can be used to stay grounded in the light when intense Scorpio energy gets too heavy.

Citrine is said to be an energetic cleanser and resonates to the sacral chakra, making it the perfect stone to have on hand to balance out Scorpio energy. Obsidian resonates with dark energy and death. Having a small piece on hand can protect one in murky situations.

Tarot Card – Death

RULES THE REPRODUCTIVE ORGANS

MUSIC NOTE – D

SACRAL CHAKRA

COLOR – MAROON

RULES INSECTS AND CRUSTACEANS

GODDESS KALI – Burn dragon's blood or copal to call upon her for support.

FLOWERS, HERBS, AND TREES

Marigold, Dragon's Blood (resin), Blackthorn Trees

ESSENTIAL OILS

Ylang Ylang – Diffuse or inhale to bring balance to the sacral chakra.

Sandalwood – Diffuse during meditation and prayer to deepen your practice and aid in transformation.

STONES

Citrine – Place on your sacral chakra to cleanse any negative energy.

Obsidian – Carry with you as a powerful ally to keep you safe and invisible around dark energies.

New Moon in Scorpio
OCTOBER 23RD TO NOVEMBER 21ST

Inventory List:

- Herb Bundle – Either store bought or to make your own see Full Moon In Capricorn Ritual Page (pg. 106)
- Matches or lighter
- Photo or photos of ancestor/s (optional)
- Candles (see below)
- Food and/or drink (see below)
- Pen and paper

New Moon in Scorpio Ritual to Honor your Ancestors

The Scorpio new moon usually takes place near Halloween, Samhain, Day of the Dead, and All Souls Day. In honor of this season, you are going to create an ancestor altar.

Ahead of time, you can gather your supplies. Get your photo or photos to display. If you do not have a photo, find something that reminds you of this person.

Gather candles – possibly in the colors and scents that the person loved. Pick or find out something that they loved eating or drinking and make sure you have it on hand. ie. chamomile tea, lemon cookies, sangria.

Designate a place for your altar and cleanse this space and yourself, by lighting your herb bundle and allowing its smoke to move around to clear any negative energies. Then say your opening invocation, see preparing for your ritual and creating sacred space (pg. 19-22).

Place the photos and items on your altar and light your candles.

Ask the person or persons you are honoring to be with you. Close your eyes and imagine them there.

Enjoy the food and/or drink that they loved. (If for any reason, you do not like or cannot consume what they loved then simply offer it to them.)

Enjoy this time and this connection.

You can ask if they have any messages for you. Listen and possibly write down any guidance you receive. Allow any part of the experience to become a sign or symbol of their presence in your life, i.e the color showing up, the scent of their favorite flower, the food or drink that they loved. Thank them for their love and support.
When you are ready, close out your sacred space (pg. 23).

Feel free to keep your altar up for as long as you like.

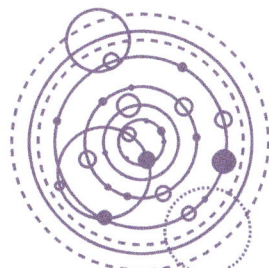

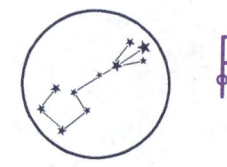

Full Moon in Scorpio
APRIL 20TH TO MAY 20TH

Inventory List:

- Herb Bundle – Either store bought or to make your own see Full Moon In Capricorn Ritual Page (pg. 106)
- Matches or lighter

Full Moon In Scorpio Ritual for Release

Begin by cleansing with your herb bundle and creating sacred space (pg. 19-22).

Then take a moment to ground yourself by taking some deep breaths through your nose.

Now that you are feeling safe and know that you are protected, it's time to be brave and take an honest look inside through all the light and happy places, deep into the darkest, hidden, scariest parts of yourself.

What is hurting you? Is it anger, resentment, sadness, frustration, fear, doubt, regret? What is the obsession within you, gnawing at you? What has got its grip on you? It could be a person, a situation, an ailment, an addiction, a belief, a job, finances, a friendship, a relationship, anything that seems out of your control. Find what it is that you are ready to let go of and leave behind in the underworld.

What is it in you that is too heavy to carry and that's no longer serving you and needs to be let go of? Find the darkness within you and spend some time sitting with it. Getting to know it. Feeling it.

After you've spent a few moments with it, it's time to make peace with it.

Repeat the following sentences out loud.

"I forgive myself for my part in this.
I release and forgive whatever parts of this situation
were outside of my doing.
I reclaim my power! I own my power!
I am powerful! I move forward fearlessly unafraid of any darkness!
I am one with all aspects of myself! I love, accept and respect all aspects of
myself! I am now free! And so it is!"

When you are ready, close out your sacred space (pg. 23).

 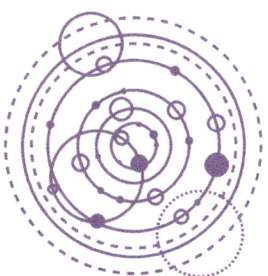

Sagittarius

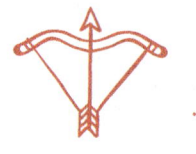 

THE SIGN OF EXPANSION
NOVEMBER 22ND TO
DECEMBER 21ST
Mutable and Fire

ADVENTURE ~ HONESTY ~ GENEROSITY ~ FAITH
THE NINTH SIGN
RULED BY JUPITER
SYMBOL – THE ARCHER
MANTRA = I SEE

Keywords:

- Expansion
- Travel
- Higher Learning
- Religion
- Philosophy
- Prayer
- Optimism
- Courts
- Ethics
- Extravagance
- Bluntness
- Overindulgence
- Outspokenness

Sagittarius season is the time of year to express joy, generosity, and optimism. It is the ninth sign of the zodiac and rules the liver, hips, and thighs. The eternal optimist of the zodiac has a "bigger is better" attitude which can, at times, get this sign into trouble.

As a mutable sign, which is also ruled by fire, Sagittarius can fan one larger-than-life creation after another; the trick is seeing it through. Ruled by Jupiter, the god of all gods,

Sagittarius is the great benevolent sign of expansion which perfectly aligns it to the third eye chakra, located in the center of the forehead, between the eyebrows. Purple, also the color associated with the third eye chakra, resonates with Sagittarius and its majestic nature.

Sagittarius, the centaur (half man-half beast), is the Latin word for "archer." The archer's arrow is the symbol and glyph for this sign.

The tarot card associated with Sagittarius is Temperance. Like the archer, using exact precision in knowing where to aim and when to shoot, the angel in this card pours water between two goblets with exact accuracy so as not to spill a drop.

Dab the essential oil of cypress on your third eye chakra and call upon Diana, the Roman goddess of the hunt, to help with aiming for your goals.

Dandelion, known as the wish granter, shares similar characteristics with the Sagittarian dynamic of bestowing favors of splendor upon its beneficiary.

Alfalfa is linked with Jupiter and is said to increase abundance and resources. Sprinkle a little under your rug to help accumulate wealth. The chestnut tree correlates to Jupiter and is said to be representative of the male reproductive organs. Chestnuts are often referred to as Jupiter's nut.

Frankincense has been used in rituals for thousands of years. It can aid in purification before setting your intentions for manifestation so that your desires come from a pure place.

The power of clear quartz can help Sagittarian energy focus on its target. It is most effective when placed on the crown of your head.

Pietersite can be placed under your pillow while you sleep to aid in the expansion of knowledge and wisdom.

Tarot Card - Temperance

RULES THE LIVER, HIPS, AND THIGHS

MUSIC NOTE - A

THIRD EYE CHAKRA

COLOR - PURPLE

RULES HORSES

Diana – Dab the essential oil of cypress on your 3rd eye chakra and call upon the Roman goddess of the hunt, to help with aiming for your goals.

FLOWERS, HERBS, AND TREES

Dandelion, Alfalfa, Chestnut

ESSENTIAL OILS

Cypress – Rub on the bottoms of your feet and lower legs when you need a motivational boost.

Frankincense – Dab on the 3rd eye chakra for clear insight from a pure conscience.

STONES

Clear Quartz – Carry or hold during meditation for clear insight.

Pietersite – Put under your pillow for expanding knowledge and consciousness.

New Moon in Sagittarius
NOVEMBER 22ND TO DECEMBER 21ST

Inventory List:

- Herb Bundle – Either store bought or to make your own see Full Moon In Capricorn Ritual Page (pg. 106)
- Matches or lighter
- Frankincense essential oil
- Carving tool
- Purple candle

New Moon in Sagittarius Ritual for Abundance

On the Thursday before this new moon, cleanse yourself by lighting your herb bundle and allowing its smoke to move around your body to clear your aura of any negative energies. Then say your opening invocation, see preparing for your ritual and creating sacred space (pg. 19-22).

Then anoint your third eye chakra with frankincense essential oil. Carve the glyph for Jupiter, ruler of Sagittarius into your candle. ♃

As you light the candle, set your intention for the gifts you'd like to have bestowed on you by the generous sign of Sagittarius.

Then repeat the words,

"I call forth the divine light of all celestial bodies to be with me now and help me to ignite my imagination so that I may see beyond what I think is possible. I call upon the great beneficent, Jupiter, the one who goes by Zeus, Ra, Thor,

and Dagda to be here with me now. Wonderful Guru, fill me with your divine knowledge of spirit, optimism, enthusiasm, abundance, prosperity, generosity, goodwill, and larger-than-life presence. I ask this not just for my own joy and inspiration, but so that I might be abundant in all good things and be able to share your benevolent spirit with all that I encounter.

On this, your day, Thor's day, I ask to be one with your realm and experience all great things manifesting all around me in every way making my life fuller and richer as I expand in consciousness and am illuminated with your wisdom and the knowing that I am constantly attracting and generating more abundance, prosperity, joy and inspiration into my life. As I feel myself completely blend with this realm, this knowing, I offer my gratitude for my deeper level of consciousness. I thank you a thousand thank yous for all the wonderful and decadent gifts you bestow upon me. Thank you Jupiter for all your blessings. And so it is."

Blow out your candle or safely allow it to go out on its own. Close out your sacred space (pg. 23).

Stellar Vibrations: Living by the Zodiac • 97

Full Moon in Sagittarius
MAY 21ST TO JUNE 20TH

Inventory List:

- Herb Bundle – Either store bought or to make your own see Full Moon In Capricorn Ritual Page (pg. 106)
- Matches or lighter
- Candle
- Pen and paper
- Cauldron, ashtray, or fire-safe container

Full Moon In Sagittarius Ritual to Remove Obstacles

There's nothing Sag wants more than to be free!

Gather your herb bundle, a pen and paper, a candle, and a lighter.

After cleansing with your herb bundle and creating sacred space (pg. 19-22), write down three big goals you have for yourself. Next to each goal, write something that you feel is standing in your way of achieving your goal.

Once you've completed your list, read aloud these words.

"I lovingly use the element of fire to transform everything and anything that blocks me from realizing the manifestation of my fullest potential.
I am ready to move forward fearlessly with faith in myself and the universe to create the best life I can live, here and now!
I am power-full!

I make things happen! I embrace change!
I am the creative director of my own life! I am in charge of myself!
I make loving choices for myself that foster my growth and potential!"

Then light your candle and use its flame to ignite your paper. Place your paper into your fire-safe container. Take a moment to feel your power and exclaim,

"So it is!"

Close out your sacred space (pg. 23) and let your candle burn as long as you like.

Capricorn

THE SIGN OF RESPONSIBILITY
DECEMBER 22ND TO
JANUARY 19TH
Cardinal and Earth

AMBITION ~ STRUCTURE ~ PRESTIGE ~ ACCLAIM
THE TENTH SIGN
RULED BY SATURN
SYMBOL – THE GOAT
MANTRA = I USE

Keywords:

- Goals
- Responsibility
- Success
- Career
- Legacy
- Recognition
- Reputation
- Profession
- Father
- Pessimism
- Public Image
- Social Status
- Grounded
- Stability

Capricorn season is the time of year where we get back to business and the focus shifts to achieving goals. The tenth sign of the zodiac marks the return of the light and the beginning of Yule with the winter solstice.

Capricorn energy is in charge of foundations and as such, it rules the foundations of the body: the bones, joints, and teeth. It is ruled by Saturn, also known as Cronos or father time, and is considered to be the mature patriarch of the zodiac, making responsibilities a priority. As a cardinal sign, which is also ruled by earth, it can lead to desires of success and recognition on one hand with mounting pressure leading to pessimism and anxiety on the other. Capricorn's earthy nature and inclination towards foundations connect this sign to the root chakra, at the base of the spine. This same earthy energy resonates with the color brown, which is also associated with Capricorn.

The Latin word, Capricornus, translates to "horned goat." Capricorn is depicted as a sea-goat, with the head of a goat and the body of a fish. The glyph for Capricorn is said to be the beard of the goat and tail of the fish.

The tarot card associated with this sign is The Devil. Like the sign of Capricorn, The Devil is horned and concerned with material needs. When feeling as though the devil is taking the lead, call upon Archangel Michael to help you regain your balance, for he is known as the biblical angel that defeats the devil.

Holly, which is associated with Yule, can be used as a decoration or placed upon the altar to welcome the light back into your life.

Juniper, with its earthy fragrance, can be used for grounding Capricorn energy. It is also known to be a mood elevator when consumed in the form of gin.

The mighty oak makes its connection to Capricorn through mistletoe, which favors the oak to all others as its preferred host.

Dab the earthy scent of patchouli on your pulse points to uplift your mood.

Create a spray with vetivert or dab the essential oil directly to the bottoms of feet for a grounding effect.

To clear the root chakra, place carnelian at the base of the spine and sit upon it as you visualize a red ball of light spinning.

Place hematite in your pocket to keep you grounded during the day and to deflect negative energy.

Tarot Card ~ The Devil

RULES THE BONES, JOINTS, AND TEETH

MUSIC NOTE – C

ROOT CHAKRA

COLOR – BROWN

RULES GOATS

Archangel Michael – Call upon to help regain your balance when feeling as though the devil is taking the lead.

FLOWERS, HERBS, AND TREES

Holly, Juniper, Oak

ESSENTIAL OILS

Patchouli – Dab this earthy scent on your pulse points to uplift your mood.

Vetivert – Create a spray by mixing 3 parts water – 1 part witch hazel or vodka – 30+ drops of vetivert in a glass spray bottle, or dab the oil on the bottoms of feet for a grounding effect.

STONES

Carnelian – Place at the base of your spine and sit upon it as you visualize a red ball of light spinning to clear the root chakra.

Hematite – Carry in your pocket to keep you grounded during the day and to deflect negative energy.

New Moon in Capricorn
DECEMBER 22ND TO JANUARY 19TH

Inventory List:

- Herb Bundle — Either store bought or to make your own see Full Moon In Capricorn Ritual Page (pg. 106)
- Matches or lighter
- Green candle
- Pitcher of water
- Planting pot
- Seeds or a starter plant
- Soil

New Moon in Capricorn Ritual to Plant Seeds for the New Year

This new moon usually occurs near the Gregorian New Year making it a great time to focus on the seeds you wish to grow and nurture in the year ahead.

Begin by cleansing with your herb bundle and creating your sacred space (pg. 19-22). Then light the green candle.

Take a moment to go within and ask your higher self, What is it that I choose to focus on this next year? Is it love? Money? Career? Family? Health?

Maybe it's more than just one thing! Be honest with yourself.

When you have a clear idea of what it is that you are ready to sow, begin playing in the soil. Let it run through your fingers. As you feel the coolness of earth in your hands, infuse it with visions of your future self. See yourself having

accomplished your goals before the year's end.

Holding on to this vision and vibration, begin to plant either your seeds or starter plant. As you plant your purpose, say:

"I (insert your name) plant my intentions for this year ahead. By the power of the Earth, I command you to grow."

Then, take your pitcher of water and as you pour it over your freshly planted goals say:

"Element of water, make it so!"

Smile and know that your new beginning has begun!

When you are ready, close out your sacred space (pg. 23).

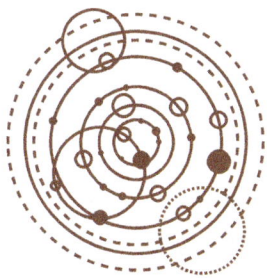

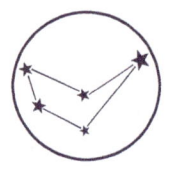

Full Moon in Capricorn
JUNE 21ST TO JULY 22ND

Inventory List:

- Fresh rosemary, garden sage, and lavender
- Twine or yarn (natural cotton)
- Flowers petals (optional)

Full Moon in Capricorn Ritual to Create an Herb Bundle

Smoke cleansing is a way to use earth energy to help clear out negative, stuck, or challenging energy in or around a space. Creating your own herb bundles for this ritual makes it even more empowering.

You can buy fresh herbs or pick them. If you are picking them, make sure it is from an area where this is allowed. You might also like to ask permission from the plant. You will receive an energetic yes or no.

You can add fresh flower petals to each bundle. Look up the energetic meaning behind the flowers to make each bundle even more special.

Begin by choosing a special place to do this ritual. Maybe outside or on a pretty tablecloth. Create your sacred space (pg. 19-22).

You will take two stems of each plant and lay them in the same direction to create a bundle about an inch thick.

Cut your twine about four times the length of your bundle. Tie the twine at the base of the stems. You will add any flower petals as you wrap. Wrap up and then

crossover back down and tie again at the base. Make sure you are wrapping your bundle tightly, as the herbs will shrink as they dry.

Once your bundle is complete you can dedicate it by saying the words,

"Precious herbs, grown by our mother,
you three become one, with the power of each other.
You cleanse, you consecrate, you balance and you heal.
Together in this bundle, it is my humble request that you honor my appeal.
Cleanse me and protect me as I believe in your magic.
Keep me safe on my journeys and at bay all that is tragic.
I honor the spirit of your sacred medicine, as I know that you are a divine gift..
And so it is!"

Close out your sacred space (pg. 23).

You can now hang your bundle upside down to dry. Where you live will depend on how long it takes to dry, but this usually takes about two weeks. The bundles must be completely dry to burn properly.

 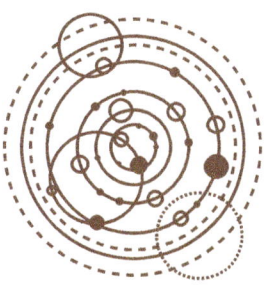

Aquarius

THE SIGN OF INNOVATION
JANUARY 20TH TO FEBRUARY 18TH
Fixed and Air

FREEDOM - INNOVATION - ECCENTRICITY - ASTROLOGY
THE ELEVENTH SIGN
RULED BY URANUS
SYMBOL – THE WATER BEARER
MANTRA = I KNOW

Keywords:

- Society
- Brotherhood
- Futurism
- Inventions
- Friendship
- Technology
- Advancements
- Space
- Surprises
- Independence
- Networking
- Collaboration
- Freedom

Aquarius season is the time of year to reinvent yourself, to break through barriers and limitations that are outdated, and to reestablish personal freedoms. It is also concerned with advancing society in the areas of science and technology. It is the eleventh sign of the zodiac and rules the circulatory system, shins, and ankles. This eccentric of the zodiac is known for rebelling against societal norms. As a fixed sign, which is also ruled by air, it can be willful and erratic at the same time.

Ruled by Uranus, the god of the universe, Aquarius holds the energy one can use to access their sixth sense. This connection to intuition stems from the third eye chakra, located on the forehead, between the eyebrows. Due to Uranus' connection to the heavens, sky blue resonates with Aquarius.

Aquarius is Latin for water carrier. The glyph for this sign is said to be the water flowing from the vessel as well as electricity and universal knowledge. The tarot card associated with this sign is The Star. Like the sign of Aquarius, The Star is depicted as a water bearer, pouring water from vessels. The water resembles streams of consciousness.

The goddess Gaia, mother of the earth, gave birth to Uranus, the god of the sky. To break through stagnant energies or situations, make an offering to Gaia by pouring some water onto the dry earth.

Wisteria is thought to promote mental clarity. Its flowers can be brewed as a tea to help sharpen intuition.

Cloves are associated with The Star card and can be used as incense or in food to sharpen psychic abilities.

Ash trees are revered as one of the oldest magical trees in existence. The wood of the tree is a preferred choice to use for making a magic wand as it is said to be a powerful resource for manifestation.

Dabbing the essential oil of jasmine on the third eye chakra aids in opening it up and can offer psychic protection. The essential oil of neroli can be used to alleviate tension and clear a cluttered mind.

Place Lapis Lazuli on the third eye chakra during a reclined meditation to help strengthen your intuition. To tap into feminine energy, imagine the energy wheel of this chakra spinning to the right and for masculine energy, imagine the energy wheel spinning to the left.

Rhodonite, like Aquarius, aids humanity through social unity. It can be carried or worn to relieve anxiety and stress.

Tarot Card - The Star

RULES THE CIRCULATORY SYSTEM, SHINS, AND ANKLES

MUSIC NOTE - A

THIRD EYE CHAKRA

COLOR - LIGHT BLUE

RULES LARGE BIRDS

GAIA - Pour some water onto the dry earth as an offering to break through stagnant energies and situations.

FLOWERS, HERBS, AND TREES

Wisteria, Clove, Ash

ESSENTIAL OILS

Jasmine – Inhale or diffuse to help uplift your mood.

Neroli – Add a few drops to a hot or cold compress to help alleviate headaches.

STONES

Lapis Lazuli – Place on the third eye during reclined meditation to help strengthen your intuition. (To tap into feminine energy, imagine the energy wheel of this chakra spinning to the right and for masculine energy, imagine the energy wheel spinning to the left.)

Rhodonite – Carry or wear to help relieve anxiety and worry.

New Moon in Aquarius
JANUARY 20TH TO FEBRUARY 18TH

Inventory List:

- Jar
- Salt
- 6 coins
- Water
- Plate

New Moon in Aquarius Ritual for Saltwater Cure

Lunar New Year begins on the date of the second new moon after the winter solstice, which always takes place in late December.

This means that the first day of the Lunar New Year can occur between January 21 and February 20.

The Lunar New year almost always falls on the New Moon in Aquarius, making this a worldwide celebrated event!

In honor of the Chinese New Year, create a saltwater cure to absorb negative energy in your home and/or office over the coming year.

Fill a jar up about 3/4ths full of salt.

Place six coins inside, heads side up. Fill the jar the rest of the way with water.

Make sure to place a plate underneath it to collect the salt that will eventually crystallize over the sides.

Top off the water regularly to keep the jar full.

The messier the jar becomes, the more negative chi or energy it is absorbing.

*Make sure to keep it out of reach from children and pets!

Full Moon in Aquarius
JULY 23RD TO AUGUST 20TH

Inventory List:

- Herb Bundle – Either store bought or to make your own see Full Moon In Capricorn Ritual Page (pg. 106)
- Matches or lighter
- Blue candle
- Jasmine essential oil

Full Moon In Aquarius Ritual to Manifest Wishes

Begin by cleansing with your herb bundle and creating your sacred space (pg. 19-22).

Then, light the blue candle and anoint your third eye chakra with jasmine essential oil.

At this point, the year is more than halfway over. Looking back to the seeds planted during the New Moon in Capricorn, take an inventory of what has manifested and what has not.

This full moon is about making wishes and has the power to make them come true! Pick one thing that stands out as most important to you.

Gently place your pointer and middle fingers from both hands on to your third eye chakra, and staring into the flame of your candle, begin to allow yourself to feel as though your wish has already manifested. With the energy of your third eye, project these feelings out into the world.

Now place your hands in prayer position close to your heart. When you are feeling this vibration the strongest, say:

"Air and ethers, water and earth, by the power of this flame I command you to make it so. Take my wish and manifest it into being with the air I blow."

Blow out your candle and say:

"I am grateful, I am grateful, I am grateful. And so it is."

When you are ready, close out your sacred space (pg. 23).

Pisces

THE SIGN OF THE MYSTIC
FEBRUARY 19TH TO MARCH 20TH
Mutable and Water

DREAMS ~ COMPASSION ~ SPIRITUALITY ~ KARMA
THE TWELFTH SIGN
RULED BY NEPTUNE
SYMBOL – TWO FISH
MANTRA = I BELIEVE

Keywords:

- Psychic Abilities
- Martyrdom
- Sleep
- Bliss
- Daydreaming
- Ecstasy
- Fantasy
- Mysticism
- Meditation
- Yoga
- Acceptance
- Addictions
- Eternity
- Reincarnation

Pisces season is the time of year to reconnect with your spiritual nature. Use caution to avoid illusions and beware of the guru. Pisces is the twelfth sign and marks the end of the zodiac.

Being that it is the last sign, it rules the feet. It is the place of escape, which can be harmless like daydreaming or meditation or extreme like addictions and altered states of consciousness. Often labeled a martyr, Pisces rules surrender and endings. As a mutable sign, which is also ruled by water, it has a go-with-the-flow attitude that, at times, can cause it to get lost in its own stream.

Ruled by Neptune, the god of freshwater, Pisces is the most spiritual of all signs and as such, it is linked to the crown chakra, located on top of the head. Due to Neptune's reign over water, the colors green and turquoise resonate with Pisces.

Pisces is the Latin word for fish and is thus the ruler of fish. The glyph for Pisces is said to be two fish tied together. The tarot card associated with this sign is The Moon. Like the sign of Pisces, The Moon is known for portraying a strong intuition and at times, can be moody and overly emotional.

Kuan Yin, the goddess of compassion can be called upon during meditation to increase love for self and others.

Water lilies, which grow by shooting up from underwater to blossom on the surface are considered to represent spiritual pursuits in which one is searching for the light. Cannabis is spiritually sacred to many cultures and can be used to alleviate stress and to alter consciousness to deepen spiritual connections.

The fig tree has a strong connection to spirituality as it is thought to be the tree under which the Buddha was sitting when he received his enlightenment.

Frankincense can be burned as incense or used as an essential oil to open the crown chakra and expand compassion. Lavender essential oil can be used before bed to enhance dream work and calm a busy mind.

Amethyst has a strong spiritual vibration that resonates with both Pisces and the crown chakra. It can be used to strengthen spiritual connections, to open and balance the crown chakra, and to overcome addictions.

Place lepidolite in a glass and insert it into a larger glass filled with water. Make sure the lepidolite does not touch the water you drink because it contains lithium and can be toxic. Place it in an area where it can absorb moonlight and drink the water the next day to help with mood imbalances.

Tarot Card – The Moon

RULES THE FEET

MUSIC NOTE – H

CROWN CHAKRA

COLOR – TURQUOISE AND GREEN

RULES FISH

KUAN YIN – Call upon during meditation to increase love for self and others.

FLOWERS, HERBS, AND TREES

Water lily, Cannabis, Fig Tree

ESSENTIAL OILS

Frankincense – Diffuse or inhale during prayer and meditation to elevate your experience.

Lavender – Inhale or add a few drops to the temples and back of the neck to open the crown chakra and alleviate worry.

STONES

Amethyst – Put under your pillow or on your nightstand to help strengthen your connection to the divine.

Lepidolite – To calm intense emotions, rub, hold or wear. You can also place it in a glass and insert it into a larger glass filled with water. Make sure the lepidolite does not touch the water you drink because it contains lithium and can be toxic. Place it in an area where it can absorb moonlight and drink the water the next day to help with mood imbalances.

New Moon in Pisces
FEBRUARY 19TH TO MARCH 20TH

Inventory List:

- Lavender essential oil
- Salt
- White candle
- Clear quartz crystal
- Herbal tea (like jasmine or rose)
- Bathtub or foot soak
- Matches or lighter

Pisces Ritual to Clear the Crown Chakra

For best results, complete one to two hours before bed. Begin by cleansing with your herb bundle and creating your sacred space (pg. 19-22). Light the candle. Then, run your bath water (or fill your foot soak) adjusting the temperature to your preference.

Pour salt into the bath along with 20 to 30 drops of the essential oil.

Once the bath is ready and before entering, place your hands over the water and say:

"I bless this water to restore my crown chakra to its proper vibration by absorbing anything that might be keeping me from feeling whole and complete."

Soak for at least 30 minutes, start with deep long breaths and ease into a relaxed breath.

When soaking, repeat the mantra "OM" aloud nine times while holding the crystal on the crown of your head. Once you have completed your bath, prepare and enjoy your tea. As you drink your tea, imagine you are drinking in pure love and say the words,

"I am one with all life and pure cosmic energy radiates through my body, mind, and soul."

When you are ready, close out your sacred space (pg. 23). Be sure to pay close attention to your dreams over the next several days, because your crown chakra is now clear, you may receive messages through them.

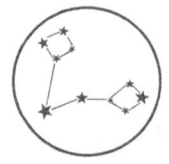

Full Moon in Pisces
AUGUST 23RD TO SEPTEMBER 22ND

Inventory List:

- Glass jar with lid
- Spring water

Full Moon in Pisces Ritual for Clarity

On the night of the full moon, cleanse yourself by lighting your herb bundle and allowing its smoke to move around your body to clear your aura of any negative energies. Then say your opening invocation, see preparing for your ritual and creating sacred space (pg. 19-22).

Fill the glass jar with spring water and sit with it under the light of the moon.

As you sit with this jar of water think about areas in your life where you would like clarity. Ask specific questions that you would like to receive answers to. Imagine how you will feel once you receive the information you seek.

Send all your energy to the water in this jar, asking it to use its powers to give you clarity.

When you feel the water has absorbed your questions, place it in the moonlight overnight and close out your sacred space (pg. 23).

The next night before going to bed, take the jar in your hands and hold it above your head and say:

"Pure water, giver of life, infuse me with the clarity of moonlight."

Drink the water down and get ready for the answers to come in the form of dreams, signs and intuitive hits.

Keep a journal to write down the information you receive. It may take a few days to make sense.

Conclusion

We hope that you enjoy using this book to help you stay connected with the celestial cycles. Connecting with these rhythms should be fun and easy and not feel like work.

Having spent the last two decades honoring the astrological energy of all the new moons and full moons, we can tell you from experience that it has linked us with our own natural rhythms and helped us to be more successful in our outer worlds and peaceful in our inner worlds. We are more linked to cosmic events than our modern world would like us to believe.

The Sun and Moon are in charge of our energetic levels and emotions. When aware of how these forces are behaving, we can better plan when to rest and recharge and when to act and make things happen.

Timing is everything and the only true mark of time on this planet is the solar year and the lunar month. We mark time by the passing and returning of these luminaries. It only makes sense that we are affected by them at a level deeper than just days on a calendar.

We wanted to make this knowledge accessible to everyone. We hope you will have fun and play with it and make these rituals your own.

LUNAR TABLES

NEW MOON

2023

MONTH	DAY	DEG	SIGN	MIN
JAN	21	01	♒	33
FEB	20	01	♓	22
MAR	21	00	♈	50
APR	20	29	♈	50
MAY	19	28	♉	25
JUN	18	26	♊	43
JUL	17	24	♋	56
AUG	16	23	♌	17
SEP	15	21	♍	59
OCT	14	21	♎	08
NOV	13	20	♏	44
DEC	12	20	♐	40

FULL MOON

MONTH	DAY	DEG	SIGN	MIN
JAN	06	16	♋	22
FEB	05	16	♌	41
MAR	07	16	♍	40
APR	06	16	♎	07
MAY	05	14	♏	58
JUN	04	13	♐	18
JUL	03	11	♑	19
AUG	01	09	♒	16
AUG	31	07	♓	25
SEP	29	06	♈	00
OCT	28	05	♉	09
NOV	27	04	♊	51
DEC	27	04	♋	58

NEW MOON

2024

MONTH	DAY	DEG	SIGN	MIN
JAN	11	20	♑	44
FEB	09	20	♒	41
MAR	10	20	♓	17
APR	08	19	♈	24
MAY	08	18	♉	02
JUN	06	16	♊	18
JUL	05	14	♋	23
AUG	04	12	♌	34
SEP	03	11	♍	04
OCT	02	10	♎	04
NOV	01	09	♏	35
DEC	01	09	♐	33
DEC	30	09	♑	44

FULL MOON

MONTH	DAY	DEG	SIGN	MIN
JAN	24	05	♌	15
FEB	24	05	♍	23
MAR	25	05	♎	07
APR	23	04	♏	18
MAY	23	02	♐	55
JUN	22	01	♑	07
JUL	21	29	♑	09
AUG	19	27	♒	15
SEP	18	25	♓	41
OCT	17	24	♈	35
NOV	15	24	♉	01
DEC	15	23	♊	53

LUNAR TABLES

2025

	NEW MOON					FULL MOON				
	MONTH	DAY	DEG	SIGN	MIN	MONTH	DAY	DEG	SIGN	MIN
	JAN	29	09	♒	51	JAN	13	24	♋	00
	FEB	28	09	♓	41	FEB	12	24	♌	06
	MAR	29	09	♈	00	MAR	14	23	♍	57
	APR	27	07	♉	47	APR	13	23	♎	20
	MAY	27	06	♊	06	MAY	12	22	♏	13
	JUN	25	04	♋	08	JUN	11	20	♐	39
	JUL	24	02	♌	08	JUL	10	18	♑	50
	AUG	23	00	♍	23	AUG	09	17	♓	00
	SEP	21	29	♍	05	SEP	07	15	♓	23
	OCT	21	28	♎	22	OCT	07	14	♈	08
	NOV	20	28	♏	12	NOV	05	13	♉	23
	DEC	20	28	♐	25	DEC	04	13	♊	04

2026

	NEW MOON					FULL MOON				
	MONTH	DAY	DEG	SIGN	MIN	MONTH	DAY	DEG	SIGN	MIN
	JAN	18	28	♑	44	JAN	03	13	♋	02
	FEB	17	28	♓	50	FEB	01	13	♌	04
	MAR	19	28	♓	27	MAR	03	12	♍	54
	APR	17	27	♈	29	APR	02	12	♎	21
	MAY	16	25	♉	58	MAY	01	11	♏	21
	JUN	15	24	♊	03	MAY	31	09	♐	56
	JUL	14	21	♋	59	JUN	29	08	♑	15
	AUG	12	20	♌	02	JUL	29	06	♒	30
	SEP	11	18	♍	26	AUG	28	04	♓	54
	OCT	10	17	♎	22	SEP	26	03	♈	37
	NOV	09	16	♏	53	OCT	26	02	♉	46
	DEC	09	16	♐	57	NOV	24	02	♊	20
						DEC	24	02	♋	14

2027

	NEW MOON					FULL MOON				
	MONTH	DAY	DEG	SIGN	MIN	MONTH	DAY	DEG	SIGN	MIN
	JAN	07	17	♑	18	JAN	22	02	♌	14
	FEB	06	17	♓	38	FEB	20	02	♍	06
	MAR	08	17	♓	35	MAR	22	01	♎	35
	APR	06	16	♈	57	APR	20	00	♏	37
	MAY	06	15	♉	43	MAY	20	29	♏	14
	JUN	04	13	♊	58	JUN	19	27	♐	33
	JUL	04	11	♋	57	JUL	18	25	♑	49
	AUG	02	09	♌	55	AUG	17	24	♒	12
	AUG	31	08	♍	06	SEP	15	22	♓	53
	SEP	30	06	♎	43	OCT	15	21	♈	59
	OCT	29	05	♏	54	NOV	14	21	♉	31
	NOV	29	05	♐	39	DEC	13	21	♊	25
	DEC	27	05	♑	50					

LUNAR TABLES

2028

NEW MOON

MONTH	DAY	DEG	SIGN	MIN
JAN	26	06	♒ Aquarius	11
FEB	25	06	♓ Pisces	21
MAR	26	06	♈ Aries	03
APR	24	05	♉ Taurus	09
MAY	24	03	♊ Gemini	41
JUN	22	01	♋ Cancer	51
JUL	22	29	♋ Cancer	51
AUG	20	27	♌ Leo	56
SEP	18	26	♍ Virgo	22
OCT	18	25	♎ Libra	16
NOV	16	24	♏ Scorpio	43
DEC	16	24	♐ Sagittarius	39

FULL MOON

MONTH	DAY	DEG	SIGN	MIN
JAN	12	21	♋ Cancer	28
FEB	10	21	♌ Leo	24
MAR	11	20	♍ Virgo	59
APR	09	20	♎ Libra	06
MAY	08	18	♏ Scorpio	44
JUN	07	17	♐ Sagittarius	02
JUL	06	15	♑ Capricorn	11
AUG	05	13	♓ Pisces	26
SEP	03	11	♓ Pisces	59
OCT	03	10	♈ Aries	59
NOV	02	10	♊ Gemini	29
DEC	02	10	♋ Cancer	24
DEC	31	10	♋ Cancer	33

2029

NEW MOON

MONTH	DAY	DEG	SIGN	MIN
JAN	14	24	♑ Capricorn	50
FEB	13	25	♒ Aquarius	01
MAR	15	24	♓ Pisces	52
APR	13	24	♈ Aries	14
MAY	13	23	♉ Taurus	05
JUN	12	21	♊ Gemini	29
JUL	11	19	♋ Cancer	38
AUG	10	17	♌ Leo	45
SEP	08	16	♍ Virgo	04
OCT	07	14	♎ Libra	48
NOV	06	14	♏ Scorpio	03
DEC	05	13	♐ Sagittarius	45

FULL MOON

MONTH	DAY	DEG	SIGN	MIN
JAN	30	10	♌ Leo	38
FEB	28	10	♓ Pisces	24
MAR	30	09	♒ Aquarius	41
APR	28	08	♏ Scorpio	26
MAY	27	06	♐ Sagittarius	45
JUN	26	04	♑ Capricorn	50
JUL	25	02	♒ Aquarius	54
AUG	24	01	♓ Pisces	12
SEP	22	29	♊ Gemini	57
OCT	22	29	♊ Gemini	16
NOV	21	29	♊ Gemini	08
DEC	20	29	♊ Gemini	21

2030

NEW MOON

MONTH	DAY	DEG	SIGN	MIN
JAN	04	13	♑ Capricorn	47
FEB	02	13	♒ Aquarius	51
MAR	04	13	♓ Pisces	44
APR	02	13	♈ Aries	12
MAY	02	12	♉ Taurus	14
JUN	01	10	♊ Gemini	50
JUN	30	09	♋ Cancer	09
JUL	30	07	♌ Leo	21
AUG	28	05	♍ Virgo	41
SEP	27	04	♎ Libra	21
OCT	26	03	♏ Scorpio	28
NOV	25	03	♐ Sagittarius	02
DEC	24	02	♑ Capricorn	57

FULL MOON

MONTH	DAY	DEG	SIGN	MIN
JAN	19	29	♋ Cancer	37
FEB	18	29	♌ Leo	38
MAR	19	29	♍ Virgo	11
APR	18	28	♎ Libra	09
MAY	17	26	♏ Scorpio	37
JUN	15	24	♐ Sagittarius	43
JUL	15	22	♑ Capricorn	41
AUG	13	20	♒ Aquarius	45
SEP	11	19	♓ Pisces	11
OCT	11	18	♈ Aries	10
NOV	10	17	♊ Gemini	47
DEC	09	17	♊ Gemini	54

LUNAR TABLES

2031

NEW MOON

MONTH	DAY	DEG	SIGN	MIN
JAN	23	02	♒	57
FEB	21	02	♓	49
MAR	23	02	♈	19
APR	21	01	♉	24
MAY	21	00	♊	04
JUN	19	28	♊	27
JUL	19	26	♋	43
AUG	18	25	♌	04
SEP	16	23	♍	43
OCT	16	22	♎	47
NOV	14	22	♏	18
DEC	14	22	♐	10

FULL MOON

MONTH	DAY	DEG	SIGN	MIN
JAN	08	18	♋	16
FEB	07	18	♌	32
MAR	09	18	♍	24
APR	07	17	♎	42
MAY	07	16	♏	25
JUN	05	14	♐	39
JUL	04	12	♑	38
AUG	03	10	♓	35
SEP	01	08	♓	46
SEP	30	07	♈	25
OCT	30	06	♉	41
NOV	28	06	♊	31
DEC	28	06	♋	46

2032

NEW MOON

MONTH	DAY	DEG	SIGN	MIN
JAN	12	22	♑	10
FEB	11	22	♓	05
MAR	11	21	♓	40
APR	10	20	♈	48
MAY	09	19	♉	29
JUN	08	17	♊	50
JUL	07	16	♋	02
AUG	06	14	♌	18
SEP	04	12	♍	52
OCT	04	11	♎	52
NOV	03	11	♏	22
DEC	02	11	♐	14

FULL MOON

MONTH	DAY	DEG	SIGN	MIN
JAN	27	07	♌	08
FEB	26	07	♍	16
MAR	27	06	♎	55
APR	25	05	♐	58
MAY	25	04	♐	28
JUN	23	02	♑	34
JUL	22	00	♒	30
AUG	22	28	♓	34
SEP	19	27	♓	00
OCT	18	25	♈	57
NOV	17	25	♉	28
DEC	16	25	♊	27

Ritual Index

A
Abundance – Page 96

B
Body Detox – Page 74

C
Celebrate with Friends – Page 80
Clarity – Page 122
Clear the Crown Chakra – Page 120
Cord Cutting – Page 82
Create an Herb Bundle – Page 106

D
Manifesting Desires – Page 64

E
Energetic Body Scan – Page 72

G
Manifest Gratitude – Page 40

H
Home Blessing – Page 56
Honor Ancestors – Page 88

I
Inner Child – Page 66

M
Making a Decision – Page 50

P
Personal Inventory – Page 32
Planting Seeds – Page 104

R
Release – Page 90
Remove Blocks – Page 98
Restoring Vitality – Page 34

S
Salt Water Cure – Page 112
Self Love – Page 42
Speaking Your Truth – Page 48
Support and Security – Page 58

W
Manifesting Wishes – Page 114

ASTROMAP

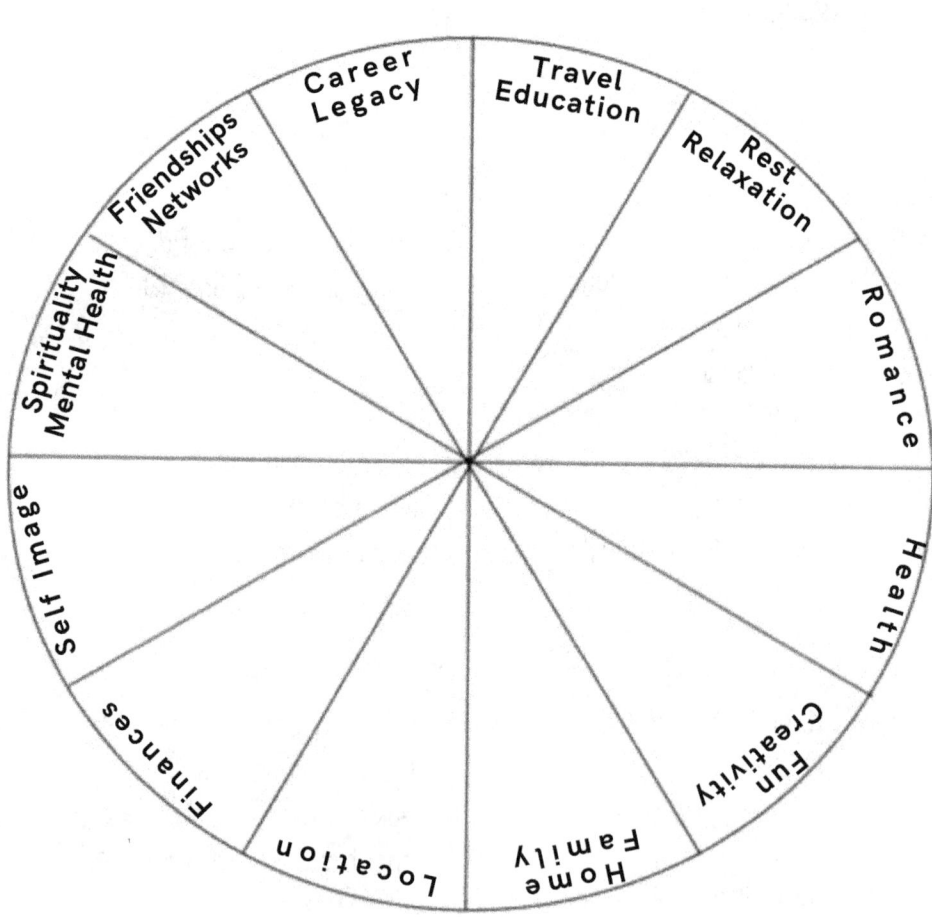

Bibliography

Beyerl, Paul (1998) The Compendium of Herbal Magic
    Phoenix Publishing

Burki, Kerry (2021) Tend To Your Vibration
    Independently published

Dean, Liz (2015) The Ultimate Guide to Tarot
    Fair Winds Press

Hall, Judy (2003) The Crystal Bible
    Godsfield Press

Sears, Kathleen (2016) Astrology 101
    Adams Media

Shaw, Paula (2013) Chakras, The Magnificent Seven
    After Midnight Press

Woolfolk, Joanna Martine (2006) The Only Astrology Book You'll Ever Need   First Taylor Trade Publishing

About the Authors

Kimberlee Marsh

Kimberlee Marsh is an astrologer, a Family Constellations Facilitator and a systemic coach with degrees in psychology and anthropology. With over 15 years of experience as an astrologer, she uses her insights to help her clients discover the divine purpose of their lives and clear out old karmic debts and ancestral entanglements. She works one on one with clients and hold numerous monthly workshops and classes both online and locally in St. Augustine Beach, Florida and she facilitates wellness retreats worldwide. Learn more at http://www.KimberleeMarsh.com

Kerry Burki

Kerry Burki is the author of the book, *Tend To Your Vibration*. She is passionate about finding unique and simple ways to help others feel good about themselves and create lives they love. She began studying spirituality in 1997 and has her B.A. in Religious Studies. Kerry is a certified yoga teacher, intuitive mentor, and magical living coach. She recently launched an apprenticeship and certification program online. She also teaches about the law of attraction at the Southwest Institute of Healing Arts in Tempe, AZ. Learn more at www.kerryburki.com

Printed in the USA
CPSIA information can be obtained
at www.ICGtesting.com
CBHW071526180724
11808CB00002B/3